CW00420844

180 Not Out

A pictorial history of cricket in
Halifax, Huddersfield, Dewsbury and District

Volume 3: South Kirklees

Compiled by Peter Davies & Rob Light

Published by Sigma Books, March 2006

First published in 2006 by:
Sigma Books, White Hollow, High Street,
East Ilsley, Newbury, Berks RG20 7LE

ISBN 0-905291-06-X

Printed and bound by:
Ridgeway Press, Pangbourne, Berks RG8 7JW

Front cover illustration: Unknown Emley CC batsman

Contents

ACKNOWLEDGEMENTS iv

INTRODUCTION v

MAP vii

1 - URBAN HUDDERSFIELD: FROM DALTON TO DEIGHTON 1

2 - LOWER COLNE VALLEY: STAR QUALITY 15

3 - WEST HUDDERSFIELD: BIRCHENCLIFFE, BIRKBY AND BAPTISTS 23

4 - ALMONDBURY: THREE FOR THE PRICE OF ONE 35

5 - UNDER CASTLE HILL: TWO FAMOUS CLUBS 43

6 - LASCELLES HALL: YORKSHIRE NURSERY 49

7 - UPPER COLNE VALLEY: PENNINE COUNTRY 56

8 - LOWER HOLME VALLEY: HONLEY AND SURROUNDS 67

9 - UPPER HOLME VALLEY: PICTURE POSTCARD LAND 79

10 - DENBY DALE AND DISTRICT: PIES AND PAVILIONS 92

11 - DEARNE VALLEY: THE VILLAGE GAME 100

12 - TOWARDS WAKEFIELD: EMLEY AND FLOCKTON 115

INDEX 121

This series of books is called '180 Not Out' on account of the fact that the first cricket club to be established in our area of research was Lascelles Hall, Huddersfield, in 1825. And it was exactly 180 years on - 2005 - when our Project came to fruition.

iii

It is more than a game,
this cricket, it somehow
holds a mirror up
to English society.
Neville Cardus

Dedication

This book, and the series as a whole, is dedicated to the wonderful people who work day and night to keep cricket alive in local communities, and to all those generous cricket folk who have helped us with our research.

Acknowledgements

We have many people to thank for their help in the preparation of this book. First, the officials of the cricket clubs and cricket leagues in the area, who have supported our work enthusiastically and passed on valuable items and images for our archive. Second, the many individuals who have supplied us with historical information and/or images – we have really appreciated this.

In terms of our colleagues, we would like to say a massive thank you to Lee Booth, Sue Brant, Andrew Hardcastle, Alex Heywood, Brian Heywood, Tim Thornton, and everyone else who has assisted us. We also owe a major debt of gratitude to the *Huddersfield Examiner, Express & Chronicle* newspapers and Kirklees Digital Photographic Archive.

Finally, an enormous thank you to the Heritage Lottery Fund and the University of Huddersfield for supporting our work financially, and Sue Burnay at Sigma Books for all her help.

Peter Davies & Rob Light, 1 March 2006

Introduction

Between 2004 and 2006 we were fortunate enough to work on a unique £50,000 Project sponsored by the Heritage Lottery Fund and the University of Huddersfield: 'The Cricketing Heritage of Calderdale and Kirklees'. Our aim was to uncover and then reconstruct the history and heritage of local cricket in Halifax, Huddersfield, Dewsbury and District.

It was a stimulating task. We staged exhibitions in towns and villages throughout the area, created an interactive cricket heritage website, recorded the memories and reminiscences of local cricket folk, manufactured cricket history-related activity packs for schools, and established an e-archive as well as two traditional archives in Halifax and Huddersfield town libraries. We worked in partnership with local libraries and museums, West Yorkshire Archive Service, local cricket leagues and local cricket clubs. We were also assisted by a wonderful Project team - students from the University and many wholehearted volunteers whose motivation was simply passion and enthusiasm for the game and its history.

We were delighted when Sigma Books said they would be interested in publishing our research in a three-volume series of photographic histories, to make our work even more accessible to the local cricket community. In this trio of books our aim has been to reconstruct and represent local cricket history pictorially through the use of a variety of sources: photographs, documents, newspaper cuttings, maps, sketches, cartoons, and many other types of images and historical items. We hope you enjoy this book – and the series as a whole.

As a geographical area, 'South Kirklees' encompasses the towns of Huddersfield, Holmfirth, Marsden, Denby Dale and also many villages and hamlets in and around. Huddersfield is obviously a major urban centre, and many of the cricket clubs located in the Huddersfield area are set against an industrial backdrop. For the most part, though, South Kirklees is a rural zone, dominated by small communities that have traditionally been linked to farming and agriculture. The fact that the BBC sitcom *Last of the Summer Wine* was filmed in and around this area is due testimony to its beauty.

The first cricket club to be founded in the area was Lascelles Hall in 1825. Thereafter, there were other significant dates. In 1842 Dalton played Sheffield for £30; in 1867 the *Huddersfield Examiner* published scores or reports on 209 matches featuring 107 different teams; in 1868 the Fartown ground was leased by Huddersfield St. Johns C.C., and in 1887 the Lumb Cup was competed for for the first time. In 1892 10 clubs joined the inaugural Huddersfield & District Cricket League competition. Over the next century we witness the birth of the Huddersfield Central League, Huddersfield Cricket Association, and many other local cricket competitions and tournaments.

Today, cricket is a central, perhaps even fundamental, part of local community life.

* * * * *

We have split this book into 12 chapters, with each focusing on one geographical zone within the umbrella area of South Kirklees. We start our journey through local cricket history in urban Huddersfield, and then move southwards to Almondbury and Lascelles Hall (the club that could plausibly lay claim to being the most famous in West Yorkshire, never mind Kirklees and Calderdale). We survey the history of cricket in three key valleys – Colne, Holme and Dearne – and finish on the fringes of Barnsley and Wakefield.

The 12 geographically-themed chapters are designed to help the reader navigate the book and the story of cricket in the area as easily as possible. There are some minor overlaps, and it would have been possible to divide the area up another way if we had wished, but we had to settle on a structure, and we feel that the one we are using is helpful. The existing clubs in the area, and their history, are our main focus, but obviously, where appropriate, we make reference to a few of the several hundred former clubs we have encountered on our travels.

Here, we would also like to recommend the other two books in this series: Volume 1 – Calderdale, and Volume 2 – North Kirklees. Together, the three books form a wonderful photographic history of cricket in this part of West Yorkshire. Please contact Sigma Books on 01635 281308 (sue@sigmabooks.fsnet.co.uk) or ourselves on 01484 472405 (p.j.davies@hud.ac.uk) if you would like to order them.

Our Project has taken us on a fascinating journey through local cricket history – the people and the places, the clubs and the leagues. And in a way, this series of three photographic histories enables us to re-live this amazing journey, and also to share it with you, the reader.

Peter Davies and Rob Light, 1 March 2006

Cricket clubs in South Kirklees, 2006

KEY

1. Almondbury CC
2. Almondbury Wesleyans CC
3. Armitage Bridge CC
4. Augustinians CC
5. Birchencliffe CC
6. Birkby FMA CC
7. Birkby Nuffield CC
8. Bradley & Colnebridge CC
9. Broad Oak CC
10. Cartworth Moor CC
11. Clayton West CC
12. Cumberworth United CC
13. Denby CC
14. Denby Dale CC
15. Edgerton CC
16. Emley CC
17. Flockton CC
18. Golcar CC
19. Hall Bower CC
20. Holmbridge CC
21. Holmfirth CC
22. Honley CC
23. Kirkburton CC
24. Kirkheaton CC
25. Lascelles Hall CC
26. Lepton Highlanders CC
27. Leymoor CC
28. Linthwaite CC
29. Marsden CC
30. Meltham CC
31. Nortonthorpe CC
32. Old Almondburians CC
33. Paddock CC
34. Primrose Hill CC
35. Scholes CC
36. Shelley CC
37. Shepley CC
38. Skelmanthorpe CC
39. Slaithwaite CC
40. Thongsbridge CC
41. Thurstonland CC
42. Upperthong CC
43. Woodfield Park CC

CHAPTER 1
URBAN HUDDERSFIELD: FROM DALTON TO DEIGHTON

Lascelles Hall aside, the oldest and most famous cricket clubs in Huddersfield tend to be, or have been, based in the urban, industrial zones: for example, Dalton, Huddersfield, Bradley Mills, Kirkheaton. And that's not forgetting other clubs of note, including Bradley & Colnebridge (who now play at Deighton), Bradley Mills WMC, Dalton Wesleyans, Deighton, Huddersfield Youth Association, Huddersfield & Lockwood, Huddersfield Clarence, Huddersfield United, Huddersfield Wanderers, ICI, Inter-Caribbean, Sheepridge & Deighton and West Indians. Urban Huddersfield was home to Fartown, where Yorkshire used to play county cricket, and was also where George Herbert Hirst and Wilfred Rhodes learnt the game.

Left: Dalton CC were formed in 1831, which makes them the second oldest club in the area. In the early years, the club produced a number of notable professional players, such as George, John and Joseph Berry, and Andrew (pictured above) and Joseph Crossland, all of whom represented Yorkshire. Right: This official DCC letter, relating to committee affairs, is dated 1885.

Struggling Dalton in dire straits

By DOUGLAS THOMSON

STRUGGLING Dalton Cricket Club could fold without an injection of fresh blood at both playing and committee level.

The warning comes from secretary Nigel Mear, who has called a special meeting at their hill-top ground on Monday (8.30).

The Drakes Huddersfield League Club really quite dire and I have to say I'm pessimistic about the future," said Mr Mear.

"We've suffered from constant vandalism and break-ins and we've been unable to open the bar, which is our only real source of income, as often as we'd have liked.

"Our only hope is that former players and any other people

Above left: An undated set of DCC rules.
Above right: A September 1991 report that hints at problems ahead. The club folded in 2003.

Although Dalton Cricket Club no longer exists, the ground on which it used to play remains in use along with its distinctive old pavilion. Edgerton Cricket Club of the Huddersfield Central League are the current lease-holders.

2

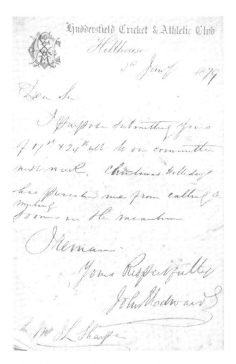

This letter dates from 1879. It was sent by officials of the Huddersfield Cricket & Athletic Club and relates to committee business.

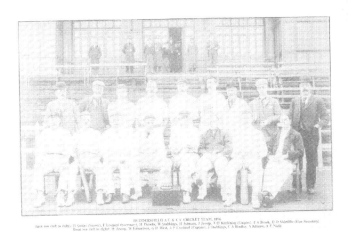

The Huddersfield side of 1896: captain A.P. Crosland (sitting, fourth from left). Sat next to him (third from left) is George Herbert Hirst.

Left: Even during wartime the club produced an annual handbook replete with facts, figures and other information. Right: Each year there was a summer festival of cricket at Fartown, home of Huddersfield CC – and a handsome programme was on sale to mark the occasion.

Huddersfield's ground at Fartown staged many county fixtures over the years. This photograph shows just how many local people took advantage to watch first-class cricket at the venue. This was Yorkshire v Somerset in May 1952.

Fartown also hosted women's county cricket. This fixture was Yorkshire v Cheshire in July 1949.

Today, the Fartown ground looks slightly dilapidated, but also, still, quite distinguished.

Left: Bradley Mills CC was located not too far away from Fartown – on the Leeds Road, close to the local heavy industry and the Huddersfield Canal. This photo was taken just after the Second World War. Right and below: W.H. 'Billy' Bolt was one of the great characters at Bradley Mills. He was a stalwart cricketer, league official, local councillor, and was fondly remembered at the club's ground.

This photo shows the hard work that went into the construction of the club's pavilion building in 1953.

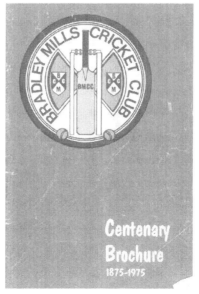

The club celebrated its 100th anniversary in 1975.

Kirkheaton CC play at Bankfield – this ground looks out over the industrial landscapes that encompass Fartown and Bradley Mills in their midst. The Kirkheaton club is most famous for its legendary cricketing sons: George Herbert Hirst and Wilfred Rhodes. As this newspaper report from 1896 makes plain, they were giant figures on the local cricket circuit.

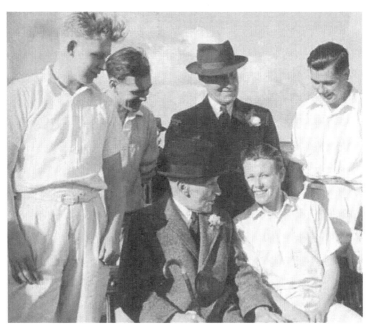

Even in later life the two men took a keen interest in their local village club.

8

BACK ROW MR WALMSLEY MR SYKES · R ROEBUCK · MR BATES
C BEDFORD · L HOWARTH · N HALLAS · R HOWARTH
R KILNER · W WADDINGTON H BROADBENT
W COWGILL · B SHEPHEARD
FRONT ROW D BUCKLEY L WOODHEAD · E · A · MᶜDONALD (CAPT) ·
G H HIRST · H WEBSTER · M · WALMSLEY
SYKES CUP 1945

This was the Kirkheaton squad that claimed the Sykes Cup trophy in 1945.

PROPOSED NEW PAVILION.

KIRKHEATON CRICKET & BOWLING CLUB
NEW PAVILION

By kind permission of the "Huddersfield Examiner."

This is the suggested design for the new cricket pavilion to be erected in honour of George Herbert Hirst
and Wilfred Rhodes. The overall dimensions are 45ft. by 30ft., with a main room of 33ft by 20ft.,
a committee room, tea room and bar.
A subscription list is open, and it is hoped to start building in the near future.

As early as 1937, the club were planning new, redeveloped premises.

9

Club members toiled long and hard to make the new pavilion building a reality.

AUGUST 26th, 1950. LAYING OF FOUNDATION STONES FOR NEW CLUBHOUSE BY GEORGE HERBERT HIRST AND WILFRED RHODES
Kirkheaton Team v Hall Bower
Back Row (l to r): S. Grange, N. Hallas, M. Walmsley, A. Lockwood, J. Laycock (Chairman), P. Earnshaw, D. Quarmby, B. Carter.
Front Row (l to r): R. Wood, G. Booth (Pro.), G. H. Hirst, H. Snow (Captain), W. Rhodes. E. Morton, L. Holt.
Sam Grange, along with Hirst and Rhodes, was a member of the 1896 Championship side.

Messrs Hirst and Rhodes were again on hand to lay the foundation stones in Summer 1950.

10

Bradley & Colnebridge CC emerged out of Colnebridge CC, who played one of their earliest fixtures in 1868.

This was the Bradley & Colnebridge team that won the Huddersfield Association Section 'B' title in 1965.

The trophy-winning Bradley & Colnebridge side of 1973: they had scooped the Lumb Cup and Huddersfield Association Section 'A' title.

Sport

Celebrations — Bradley and Colnebridge are pictured in front of their pavilion at Warrenside as they celebrate 40 years since their re-formation. The club have come on in leaps and bounds since the dark days of 1994 when they were forced to quit their Colnebridge base, and they can be justifiably proud of their new headquarters. Back row (from left), Joanne Atkinson (scorer), Andy Barber, Ian Richardson, Tim Stead, Owen Atkinson, Dave Moorhouse, Dave Pickure, Dave Senior, (front) Steve Jackson, Raymond Hawley and (chairman), Steve Ashwell, Kevin McAvenue (founder member), Graham Simpkins, Steve Fisher.

Perseverance pays off

IF EVER proof was needed that perseverance pays off, then you would need look no further than Bradley and Colnebridge.

The NTL Central League Section B side are now putting all their recent problems behind them and this season celebrate 40 years since their re-formation, highlighted by the capture of a new pitch at the Huddersfield Hotel complex, who are

Bradley and Colne in celebratory mood

NTL Central League: DAVID LOCKWOOD

After additional work on the ground involving laying of land drains, re-seeding and putting 350 tons of top soil on Warrenside, Bradley started life at their new premises in April 1996 – but without a pavilion.

A National Lottery grant helped them fund the building of a pavilion, which was opened by the late Alec Lodge in August 1997 and Bradley gained their first real boost by lifting the Section C title.

In 1999 B&CCC celebrated their 40th anniversary – against the backdrop of their new pavilion building at Warrenside, Deighton.

12

Lumb Cup winners for first time

The West Indians, who, playing in the final for the first time, won the Lumb Cup (Huddersfield's oldest cricket trophy) during the week, beating Rastrick New Road in the final. Back row—R. Maximen (scorer), W. Wood (umpire), J. Maximen, R. Gordon, B. Hale, S. Lewis, A. McPherson, O. Kallman, J. W. McColman, S. Ashton (umpire). Front row—C. Gill, E. Webster, S. Inniss, W. Welch, S. Chester.

Fine innings by captain for winners | **CROSSLAND TROPHY** *Oakes win a low-scoring game* | **GOLF** Balderstone shines in Longley wir

THE West Indians gained a fine victory in the Hudders

In the post-war years, Huddersfield welcomed immigrants from Asia and the Caribbean. West Indian CC were the first predominantly ethnic side to scoop a major trophy – the Lumb Cup in 1963.

Cricket exhibition, Tolson Museum, Huddersfield

CRICKET history is on show in Huddersfield.
Treasured items from the sport's past are on display at the Tolson Museum, Moldgreen, all summer.
England women's cricketer Clare Taylor was among the first visitors who got to see scorecards, match balls, photos and newspaper cuttings depicting the development of the area's clubs.
The exhibition springs from a pioneering cricket heritage project launched at Huddersfield University with a £43,000 grant from the Heritage Lottery fund.
It is 180 years since Lascelles Hall became the first Huddersfield cricket club in 1825. Since then, 58 other clubs have been formed.
Former cricketers who gathered at the exhibition's opening included England Test player Eddie Leadbeater, who played for Almondbury, and Stanley Inniss, a Caribbean who came to Huddersfield from Barbados in the 1950s and became a JP and was awarded the MBE for his community work.
The exhibition has been put together by Dr Peter Davies, from the university, and his colleague Rob Light. It includes a large-scale Owzat game, cricket gear to try on and a card game featuring cricketing greats from the Kirklees area.

HOWZAT: Looking at some of the exhibits are Eddie Leadbeater (left) and Stanley Inniss, and (right) organisers Peter Davies (left) and Rob Light with England women's cricketer Clare Taylor

Stanley Inniss came to Huddersfield from the Caribbean in the post-war years and has played a key role in local cricket ever since. He is now a JP and involved in the Kirklees Race Relations Board. He was a VIP guest at the opening of a special cricket heritage exhibition at the Tolson Museum, Huddersfield in 2005.

Two other Huddersfield teams: 'United' and 'Wanderers', who both played fixtures around the turn of the twentieth century. (Below: Wilfred Rhodes is standing second from right and George Herbert Hirst is second from the right on the front row).

THE HUDDERSFIELD WANDERERS
Back row from left: Lawrence Hirst, Hubert Smith, Leonard H Beaumont, Scorer, W E D Shaw, Wilfred W Rhodes, Joseph Hall (Umpire)
Front row from left: Schofield Haigh, Tom Hudson, Harold Shaw, Harry Schofield (Captain), Edgar Walker, George H Hirst, Harold H Ramsden
PLAYED AT GOLCAR SEPTEMBER 26th 1903

CHAPTER 2
LOWER COLNE VALLEY: STAR QUALITY

The lower Colne Valley encompasses three existing cricket clubs (Paddock, Golcar, Leymoor) and many other ex-clubs (for example, Paddock CYC, Paddock CYC OB, Paddock Institute, Gentlemen of Golcar, Golcar Church Institute, Golcar Liberal, Golcar Treasurer's XI, Milnsbridge Baptists, Milnsbridge CYC, Milnsbridge Wesleyans). It is a raw but spectacular part of Huddersfield, choc-a-bloc with terraced houses and breathtaking panoramas of the valley. The cricket grounds of the area have been graced by some of the greatest international stars of all time, including Gary Sobers and Sonny Ramadhin.

Paddock Cricket & Bowling Club was formed by a group of young men from Paddock Methodist Church in 1872. The club was originally called Paddock Rangers and only played rugby. But, by the middle of the 1870s, cricket had been introduced. This meant a suitable field had to be found. Consequently, three grounds were used before the lease agreement above with John Foster of Gledholt secured the current ground, West View, in 1882.

In this 1921 photograph Paddock 2nd XI show off their club caps and blazer. Two years later the 1st XI was victorious in the Sykes Cup final for the first time. The *Huddersfield Examiner* gave this vivid account of the team's return home following the victory: 'A huge crowd awaited the arrival of the charabanc at Longroyd Bridge, and to the martial strains of *See the Conquering Hero Comes*, played *con brio* by the Milnsbridge Socialist Band, the party proceeded up the village.'

Paddock Cricket & Bowling Club has a proud record of grooming future Test cricketers. After beginning his career at Oakes Council School, Percy Holmes first emerged as a cricketer of note while playing for Paddock. In 1911, just two years before his Yorkshire debut, he won the Huddersfield League batting prize while playing for the club. A second future Yorkshire and England cricketer enjoyed early success with Paddock in 1937 - Willie Watson (pictured above).

In 1955, two decades after Willie Watson had first made his name with the club, a third future England Test cricketer broke into the Paddock 1st XI - Chris Balderstone, who is pictured here (front row, far left).

At the start of the next decade, the great West Indian all-rounder Gary Sobers played for the club as a substitute professional. This photograph was taken during his first appearance, which came against Elland at Whitsuntide in 1962.

West View from the air. Note the proximity of the railway and the rows of terraced housing nearby.

Golcar Cricket Club was founded as St. John's Golcar Cricket Club in 1871, the name reflecting links with the nearby church. In 1905 the traditional Golcar Sing took place on the club's Town End ground.

18

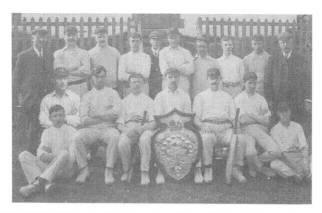

In the last decades of the nineteenth century, Golcar Cricket Club was instrumental in founding Huddersfield's first three modern cricket institutions. In 1886 the club became a founder member of the Huddersfield Cricket Association. It took part in the first Lumb Cup competition in the following summer, and five years later the club joined the town's inaugural league competition, the Huddersfield & District Cricket League. Success in the League followed at the start of the next century, as the Byrom Shield was won in 1903 and 1905 (above).

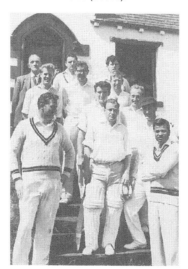

During the 1950s and 1960s the Huddersfield League restricted each club to only one professional player. However, if the contracted professional was not available for any match a substitute could be engaged to take his place. In 1963 this led to West Indian Test star Sonny Ramadhin appearing for Golcar when regular professional Peter Eyre was unavailable. In four matches that season, Ramadhin (pictured above with his Golcar teammates) took 27 wickets for 92 runs as the club reached the Sykes Cup final. Unfortunately, he was not available for the final, which rivals Paddock won by 7 wickets.

19

In 1988 the club scooped a trip to Lord's after qualifying for the final stages of a national six-a-side tournament.

Links between Golcar Cricket Club and the Caribbean did not end with Sonny Ramadhin. Since 1992 the club has run bi-annual tours to Barbados, with a reciprocal tour to West Yorkshire from the North Stars club also taking place in recent years. This photograph shows Golcar's 2000 touring party enjoying the Caribbean cricket experience.

Leymoor United are the 'other Golcar club', situated just down the road. The club played in the Colne Valley League circa 1900 and then moved into the Huddersfield Central League. Like many clubs they went into hibernation around the time of the Second World War, but re-formed in 1950. The photo above was taken at their first match as a reconstituted club.

Leymoor are well known for their thriving junior set-up. This group of Under-13s were local champions in 1995.

Leymoor have a unique community link. The Colne Valley is very much brass band territory, and their clubhouse is the HQ of the Golcar Band.

Leymoor's ground is also famous for its location. A pub – the Walkers Arms – lies adjacent to the boundary at the bottom end, and locals enjoy nothing more than watching the cricket, while drinking, on summer Saturdays.

CHAPTER 3
WEST HUDDERSFIELD: BIRCHENCLIFFE, BIRKBY AND BAPTISTS

'West Huddersfield' connotes the suburbs served by the main roads to Rochdale and Halifax (New Hey Road and Halifax Road). It is very much an urban zone, full of houses, factories, schools and churches, and centres on Birkby, Marsh, Edgerton, Lindley, Birchencliffe, Oakes and Salendine Nook. Because it is such a built-up area, there are not that many 'green spaces', and many cricket clubs in the area have gone out of business - for example Acre Mills CC, Birkby CYC CC, Birkby St. John's CC, Birkby United CC, Lindley CC, Lindley Church CC, Marsh CC, Martins CC, Oakes Baptists CC, Oakes CYC Old Boys CC and Pole Moor CC. Most existing clubs in the area do not have a long history.

One of the early clubs in the area was Salendine Nook Baptists. This is an extract from the Baptists' scorebook, which records the details of one innings from a 2nd XI local derby against Oakes in 1897. It is not clear whose innings it is, but the scorebook goes on to say the game was played at 'Cowrakes'. Needless to say, there is no sign of a cricket ground on Cowrakes Road today – it is all modern housing. In 1913 Salendine Nook Baptists were founder members of the Huddersfield Central Cricket League but only survived until 1917, when the dislocation of war forced them out of business.

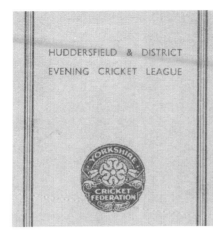

HUDDERSFIELD & DISTRICT
EVENING CRICKET LEAGUE

Bowled over

A CRICKET CLUB has won a cash windfall in latest lottery handouts. The Salendine Nook Old Boys Cricket Club at Salendine Nook High School has been granted £3,998 by the English Sports Council. The money will go towards a project to install an artificial cricket wicket, set to cost £5,198 in all. Eight awards, totalling £1.8m, were made to organisations in Yorkshire.

Salendine Nook has seen its fair share of cricket clubs come and go. The latest to fold, in 2005, was Salendine Nook Old Boys (SNOBs), a club formed three decades previously. Over the years it had put out teams in the Huddersfield Association, Huddersfield Evening League, Huddersfield Central League and the Halifax League.

Salendine Nook OB before their 10-wicket rout of Old Almondburians "B," line-up—Back (from left): Laura Galvin (scorer), John Normanton, Mark Doyle, Neil Whiteley, Billy Waddington, Mick O'Neil (captain), Mike Shorthose. (Front) Mike Dixon, Mick Walker, Chris Fox, Andy Deighton and Chris Walker

SNOBs CC in 1989.

Part of the team: The tea lady at the Old Boys' New Hey Road ground.

Britannia Works C.C. played on a field only a few hundred yards away from SNOBs' HQ. They joined the Huddersfield Association in the early 1930s. In the decades that followed they won an array of silverware, including the Lumb Cup, Challenge Shield, Crossland Trophy and Sharpe Rose Bowl. Early on, there were quite strict rules about who could play for the club – they had to belong to the Britannia Works Sports Club. Britannia's most famous players included Leslie Chatterton and Jock MacLean. The club folded in the post-war years. Several clubs have 'lodged' at the Britannia Works ground in recent years, including Harry Lime CC, Edgerton CC and Birkby FMA CC.

Birkby Former Members Association captain Richard Blacker receives the Section II championship trophy from Mrs Margaret Tyas, wife of the Cricket Association secretary Peter Tyas, as members of the winning team look on.

Birkby FMA (Former Members' Association) was founded in 1965 by Jerry Smith (captain-to-be), Colin Brennan and a group of friends. Birkby FMA joined the Huddersfield Association League in 1965. This photo shows them claiming the Association Section 'B' title in 1981.

LUMB CUP

FINAL

Birkby FMA

V

International

WOODFIELD PARK SUNDAY 13TH AUGUST 1989

ADULTS 50P   CHILDREN AND OAP'S 25P

In 1989 the club reached the final of the prestigious Lumb Cup – only to be pipped at the post by International CC.

Like many other local clubs, Birkby FMA is a family affair: Bryan Dolley (left) and Allan Dolley (right) have been long-time players, while Julie Dolley is a key administrator.

Results to date.
First Elevens.

	P.	W.	L.	D	Pts
Honley Wesleyans	15	13	1	1	27
Lepton Highlanders	15	11	2	2	24
Milton Church	15	8	5	2	18
Cowcliffe Church	16	8	6	1	17
Rastrick New Road	15	7	6	2	16
Oakes Baptist	16	6	6	3	15
Almondbury Wesleyans	16	6	8	1	13
Bradley and Colnebridge	16	6	8	1	13
Outlane	16	6	9	1	13
Blackley	15	5	9	1	11
Leymoor	16	3	10	3	9
Y.M.C.A.	16	3	11	2	8

Second Elevens.

Cowcliffe Church	16	13	2	1	27
Lepton Highlanders	16	11	4	1	23
Outlane	16	10	3	3	23
Honley Wesleyans	16	8	7	1	17
Oakes Baptist	16	8	7	1	17
Rastrick New Road	16	7	7	2	16
Almondbury Wesleyans	16	7	8	1	15
Blackley	16	6	9	1	13
Leymoor	16	6	9	1	13
Milton Church	16	4	10	2	10
Bradley and Colnebridge	16	4	11	1	9
Y.M.C.A.	16	2	13	1	5

YMCA CC was founded in the early twentieth century, and in 1923 they were struggling in both sections of the Huddersfield Association.

Lumb Cup Winners For The First Time

The Y.M.C.A. cricketers who won the Lumb Cup for the first time in their history by beating Brook Motors by a narrow margin in the final at Woodfield Park on Saturday. Back row: S. Ashton (umpire), E. Heaton, G. Hancock, E. Dunn, J. T. Sykes, J. Gibson, S. Dyson, I. Pell (umpire). Front row: R. Bray, M. V. Robinson, F. Gilleard (capt.), E. Hirst, A. Young.

BOWLING
M....... C:...:

In 1956 YMCA CC scooped the Lumb Cup. Notice the presence of the two club umpires on the back row of this team photo.

YMCA CC has a claim to being the first multi-cultural cricket club in Huddersfield. Star performers of the 1980s and 1990s were Riaz Iqbal (left), of Pakistani descent, and Dr Gunasiri Ambepitia (right), a Sri Lankan doctor.

28

Like some other clubs in the area, YMCA CC have published their own internal club newsletter.

Highfields was an old municipal ground close to the town centre. Edgerton CC, in the Huddersfield Association, were one of the many local clubs to play their home games at the venue.

Edgerton C.C. was founded in 1981 by cricket enthusiasts Johnny Bradbury and Barry Snowden. They wanted to call themselves the 'Huddersfield Vagabonds' but this was rejected by the Huddersfield Association. Eventually, at a key meeting, club representatives were told to leave the room...and Association reps chose the name 'Edgerton' for the new club on account of their HQ at Highfields, Edgerton. This is an early team photo.

EDGERTON F.M.A. - 1993

May the Thirtieth, Nineteen ninty three.
The Edgerton tour organised by Johnny 'B'.
Beeford & Leven were to be the hosts.
As we go to East Yorkshire - on the Coast.
Not many instructions did Johnny 'B' leave.
But Stuart did a factsheet to our relief.
And t'tour began proper - wi'out any qualms.
At noon, at Beeford, at t' Tiger Arms.
Then to the match, down Recory Lane.
Park in a paddy field & avoid the rain.
Yes same problems as last year-a force 10 gale,
and Beeford C.C. don't sell ale.

The club went on an annual tour every summer – a tradition that gave rise to this piece of poetry.

We've won the cup!

Augustinians Cricket Club celebrated their victorious season in the Huddersfield Association Cricket League with a dinner-dance at the Shambles Restaurant. The first team won the Section "A" championship and one of the guest speakers, Police team captain Insp Peter Bottomley (left), presented the trophy to Augustinians captain Harold Ainley

Augustinians CC are another club who played their formative years in the Huddersfield Association. This pair of successes – above in 1981 and below in 1983 – led to them being christened the 'team of the '80s'.

Cup Kings reign despite the rain

Once again it's been a highly successful season in the Huddersfield Cricket Association, believes president John Harold. That's because his Augustinians side have clinched a hat-trick of Section "A" titles. Augustinians captain Harold Ainley is pictured receiving the Combination Challenge Cup from league fixtures secretary Peter Bottomley before Saturday's final programme, which was a complete wash-out

31

The club play their home fixtures at Laund Hill, in the grounds of the Lawrence Batley Sports Centre, close to Junction 23 of the trans-Pennine M62.

In winter, rugby posts are erected, but the cricket sightscreen is still visible.

32

During the inter-war years Birchencliffe Church flew the flag for the village in the Huddersfield Association. They won the 2nd XI league – and knockout competition – in 1934.

The Church side folded during the Second World War, but a new club – Birchencliffe CC – was established in 1950 by patrons at the Royal Hotel in the village. This cutting shows that they performed particularly well in the summer of 1957.

insert
redale

Insert
T. Robinson

WINNERS 1958

G. Plant, S. Sykes, N. Barrowclough, A. McGinty, D. Greaves, J. Keegan, W. Ingleby, L. Powel
G. Mullins, G. Hinchcliffe, R. Clay (Captain), S. Pickering, B. Liley.

They were successful again in 1958…

…and today they are a thoroughly professional outfit, with players and officials wearing club tracksuits to all functions and events, like this cricket heritage exhibition in 2005.

CHAPTER 4
ALMONDBURY: THREE FOR THE PRICE OF ONE

Almondbury has a claim to being the ultimate South Kirklees cricket village. It boasts three clubs – Almondbury CC, Almondbury Wesleyans CC and Old Almondburians CC – and another cricketing outfit that confines itself to friendly fixtures: Almondbury Casuals (according to the ACCC website: 'The Almondbury Casuals was first formed in apparently 1949 A.D. in the Wool Pack Hotel, Almondbury, Huddersfield by a group of boozed-up chaps who had run out of conversation. Thus from this humble beginning was born a Cricket Club which over the next 37 years has by dint of honest endeavour advanced not a bit, but remains the glorious shambles that it is today. Nevertheless a team has turned out regularly on every Sunday in the summer made up of essentially modest players who have a lot to be modest about. However, it can be said that our playing record shows that over the years we have won at least half our matches though no-one seems to know how'). The setting is attractive too. Almondbury is a desirable and historic settlement, with a celebrated parish church (which also once had a cricket team) and a plethora of fashionable bistros and wine bars. It is also famous for Castle Hill – the landmark that is synonomous with Huddersfield as a town and offers the visitor an amazing panoramic view of Pennine country.

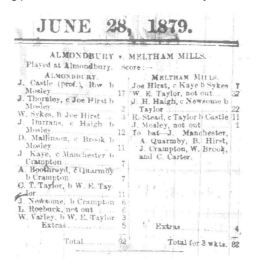

Almondbury CC was founded by a group of local cricket enthusiasts who had played in the vicinity in 1873. By 1879 the club was playing fixtures against established teams like Meltham Mills. It was also employing a professional – J. Castle, an opening bat.

On 24 November 1874 the club acquired a lease for Fernside Avenue, and has played there ever since.

The club's most famous son is leg-spinner Eddie Leadbeater, who played Test cricket for England in the 1950s.

The Almondbury side that won the Sykes Cup for the first time in 1962.

HECKMONDWIKE CRICKET CLUB

*

HEAVY WOOLLEN DISTRICT
CRICKET CHALLENGE CUP FINAL

SUNDAY, 15TH AUGUST, 1976
WICKETS PITCHED 2.00 P.M.

*

ALMONDBURY
versus
OSSETT

*

ADMISSION : ADULTS 25p
OLD AGE PENSIONERS & CHILDREN 10p

Perhaps the club's most notable success came in the 1976 Heavy Woollen Cup final. When Ossett were defeated by 10 runs, Almondbury became the first Huddersfield-based side to win the famous old trophy since Lascelles Hall in 1891.

Club women in the new Fernside Avenue tea room in the 1970s.

FIRST ELEVEN.					SECOND ELEVEN.		
Date.	Name of Club.	At	Rlt.		Date.	Name of Club.	At	Rlt.
1909					1909			
May 1					May 1			
8	Rastrick	away			8	Rastrick	home	
15	Cowcliffe Church	home			15	Cowcliffe Church	away	
22	Brighouse Park Ch.	home			22	Brighouse Park Ch.	away	
29	Hillhouse U.M.C.	away			29	Hillhouse U.M.C.	home	
June 5	*Skelmanthorpe Prim.	away			June 5	*Skelmanthorpe Prim.	home	
12	Huddersfield Mission	home			12	Huddersfield Mission	away	
19					19			
26	Rastrick	home			26	Rastrick	away	
July 3	Cowcliffe Church	away			July 3	Cowcliffe Church	home	
10	Brighouse Park Ch.	away			10	Brighouse Park Ch.	home	
17	Hillhouse U.M.C.	home			17	Hillhouse U.M.C.	away	
24	Huddersfield Mission	away			24	Huddersfield Mission	home	
31	*Skelmanthorpe Prim.	home			31	*Skelmanthorpe Prim.	away	
Aug. 7					Aug. 7			
14					14			
21					21			
28					28			
Sept. 4					Sept. 4			
11					11			
18					18			
	* Ordinary Match.					* Ordinary Match.		
	Sheepridge League.					Sheepridge League.		

Almondbury Zion CC was the forerunner of Almondbury Wesleyans CC, having occupied the Kaye Lane ground until 1910. The club played in the Sheepridge & District League before the First World War. This is an extract from their 1909 membership booklet.

ALMONDBURY WESLEYAN C.C.
Back Row (L to R) Harry Stell, Wm Arthur Crowe, Arthur Haigh, Hamer Lockwood
Ernest Armitage (Scorer) Middle Row (L to R) Arthur Wood, Ernest Hickman, Harold Crawshaw
Joe Sheard, Charlie Dawson. Front Row (L to R) Stanley Dawson, John Charles Shaw
1921

The current cricket club was formed as part of the Almondbury Wesleyan Athletic Club in November 1920, and 1921 was its first full season.

Membership cards from the 1930s.

39

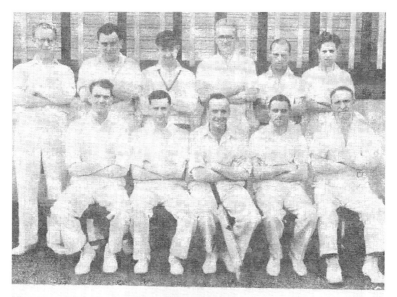

Back Row:—F. Worth, P. Gronow, F. Greenhalgh, S. Cooper, F. Brook, J. M. Dyson.
Front Row:—J. Branston, J. W. Branston, E. Holt (Capt.), L. Sowden, T. Nestor

The 1953 side that bagged the Huddersfield Association title and the Lumb Cup.

In recent years the club has been transformed following a lottery grant which enabled the redevelopment of the Kaye Lane facilities. As well as a new state-of-the-art pavilion, the playing surface was levelled and practice nets provided. The new premises were opened by Yorkshire and England legend Brian Close in 2002.

The new Kaye Lane pavilion

Although Old Almondburians CC was not formed until 1976, King James School had been using the Arkenley Lane ground for cricket during the previous 92 years. The club was formed by the Old Almondburians' Society, a fellowship of past pupils and staff of the School. Fittingly, the School 'Old Boys' celebrated the 100th anniversary of cricket being played at the ground in 1984. Jack Taylor – a legendary bowler at the club – is in the middle of this gathering.

R. Dowling's drawing of the Arkenley Lane pavilion.

Old Almondburians'
Cricket Club

Annual Dinner
&
Presentation
Evening

Longley Park Golf Club
Saturday 29th October 2005.
6.30pm for 7.00pm

Chairman: J. A. Taylor

On behalf of the President and the committee of the
O.A.C.C may I, as Chairman,
extend a very warm welcome to our
Guests, Old Almondburians, Club members
and their partners.

The big event of 2005.

CHAPTER 5
UNDER CASTLE HILL: TWO FAMOUS CLUBS

The Victoria Tower – known simply as Castle Hill – is the most significant landmark in South Kirklees. It is perched high above Huddersfield town centre and attracts its fair share of visitors in summer – mainly walkers, photographic enthusiasts and kite-flyers. It looks down on two longstanding Huddersfield League cricket clubs: Hall Bower CC and Primrose Hill CC.

Looking down from Castle Hill on Hall Bower's ground.

HALL BOWER v. MOLDGREEN. — This match was played on the ground of the former, on Saturday last, and resulted in a victory for the home team. Score :—
HALL BOWER.—J. E. Haigh 11, H. Lodge 6, J. Lodge 1, Thornton 0, Liversedge 1, T. Haigh 3, Moorhouse 0, Maffin 6, Tiffany 0, Calvert (not out) 0, Matthewman 0, extras 2; total 30.
MOLDGREEN.—Mallinson 0, Woodcock 0, Armitage 8, Halstead 2, Eastwood 0, Mosley 2, Brook 0, Fulcher 4, Boothroyd (not out) 1, Howarth 0, Price 0 ; total 17.

Formed in the previous year, Hall Bower Cricket Club played their first fixture at Castle Hill on 14 April 1877 against Moldgreen. This is how the low-scoring match was reported in the *Huddersfield Examiner*.

This photograph was taken in the late 1890s. At this time the club competed in the Huddersfield Alliance League, which it had helped to found in 1893. In 1913 the club left the Alliance to become founder members of the Huddersfield Central Cricket League.

The 'tea tent' in the 1950s.

Hall Bower left the Central League in 1940 to join the Huddersfield & District Cricket League. However, success in the League's major knockout competition proved elusive and it was not until 1972 that the club enjoyed a Sykes Cup final victory. Here the victorious captain Geoff Heywood shows the trophy to Harold Parkin.

A lot on his plate – former Huddersfield striker Andy Booth, now with Sheffield Wednesday, is playing cricket for Hall Bower

Playing cricket under the Hill

A PLATE depicting Castle Hill and Hall Bower is available from a local cricket club.

Hall Bower Cricket Club has commissioned 350 of the plates from local artist Jenny Hinchliffe and

The plates, each costing £15, were commissioned during the summer when the club enjoyed an excellent season on its return to Section A of the Drakes Huddersfield League.

The illustrated plates are available by contacting club treasurer Glyn

The club's most famous member is Huddersfield Town – and ex-Tottenham – centre-forward Andy Booth.

Primrose Hill Cricket Club began life in 1875. In the early days, they were known by other monickers: the 'Hillites', the 'Pip Hillers', and the 'Pips'. In 1891 the Lumb Cup was won and in the following year Primrose Hill became founder members of the Huddersfield & District Cricket League. However, in 1908, only three years after this photograph was taken, they lost their place in the League, not regaining it until 1920.

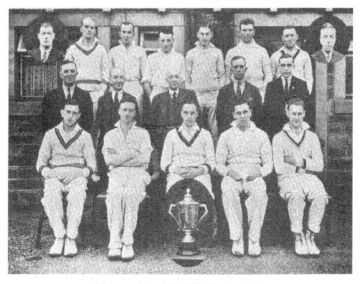

Winners of the Hinchliffe Cup in 1934.

A team photograph taken in June 1953.

Left: Legendary supporter Polly Ball.
Right: Ken Taylor was a future Test batsman in the making when he turned out for
Primrose Hill. He was also a talented artist.

Club officials hoist the Centenary flag in 1975.

The Ladies' Committee

Mrs. Dawson   Mrs. Evans   Mrs. Tipling
Mrs. Turner   Mrs. Haley   Mrs. Kaye

The women of the Primrose Hill club in the 1970s.

CHAPTER 6
LASCELLES HALL: YORKSHIRE NURSERY

If one South Kirklees club is deserving of its own chapter in this book, it is Lascelles Hall. The club is not just the oldest in Huddersfield (1825) but in the mid-nineteenth century it supplied many cricketers to the Yorkshire county team and the England national side. The origins of cricket in the village – and today it is more hamlet than village – are tied up with the owner of the local hall, Lascelles Hall. In a noble gesture she allowed local weavers to play cricket on the field – in essence to keep them occupied and happy.

Sheffield (Bramall Lane) v. Lascelles Hall for £50 aside, 19th, 20th, 21st September, 1870.

LASCELLES HALL.

1st Innings		2nd Innings	
J. Brook, c West b Cuttell	7		
W. Shotton, b West	5		
A. Greenwood, c Pinder b Armitage	43	lbw Armitage	0
E. Lockwood, c Pinder b West	8	thr. out, Pinder	3
D. Eastwood, b West	40	b West	35
L. Greenwood, c Cuttell b Armitage	11	not out	35
Jno. Thewlis, b Cuttell	45	not out	6
Jno. Ambler, b West	8		
D. Pollard, not out	0	c Pinder b Armitage	3
A. Hill, c and b West	6	c Stephenson b West	0
T. Redfearn, st. Pinder b Cuttell	29		
Extras	2	Extras	2
	210	For 5 wickets	84

10

SHEFFIELD.

1st Innings		2nd Innings	
C. Webster, b Pollard	5	c and b L. Greenwood	5
T. Brownhill, c Hill b L. Greenwood	46	c L. Greenwood b Hill	11
E. Stephenson, b Hill	0	not out	56
G. Thorpe, c and b Hill	2	lbw Lockwood	4
J. Rowbotham, b L. Greenwood	10	run out	23
G. Pinder, c Hill b Greenwood	22	b Pollard	12
W. Cuttell, c Ambler b Greenwood	1	b Eastwood	21
J. West, b Hill	3	b Lockwood	8
E. Ryalls, not out	6	c and b Lockwood	0
T. Armitage, b L. Greenwood	0	c Greenwood b Eastwood	34
J. Rodgers, b Hill	3	c Thewlis, b Lockwood	6
Extras	8	Extras	5
	106		185

This is the scorecard of one of the earliest stake matches. It was played at Bramall Lane, Sheffield, where Yorkshire once played and Test matches were held too. The fact that a small village side (Lascelles Hall) was taking on the might of a big-city team (Sheffield) is adequate testimony to the pedigree of the legendary LHCC.

49

Lascelles Hall in the nineteenth century was home to an array of cricketing pioneers including Billy Bates (above left), Allen Hill (above right), John Thewlis (below left) and Ephraim Lockwood (below right).

LASCELLES HALL XI. (Winners of the Heavy Woollen District Challenge Cup, 1891.)

John Eastwood (Representative). W. Pollard. C. H. Milnes. A. P. Crossland. John Thewlis. Harry Bates. Walter Kaye. R. Clayton (Sec.). Joe Wright (Scorer).
David Lockwood. Alf. Thewlis. W. Bates. Walter Haigh (President). John Haigh. Eph. Lockwood. Herbert Thewlis. L. Broadhead.

Lascelles Hall stormed to victory in the 1891 Heavy Woollen Cup final, and the red letter day was commemorated in a special piece of music.

51

The club carnival was a colourful date in the annual calendar, particularly in the first decade of the last century.

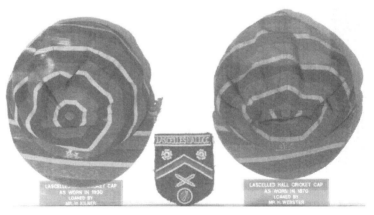

The Lascelles Hall club cap is also highly colourful (purple, cream and black), and has changed little over the decades. Here the 1870 version (right) is contrasted with that of 1930 (left).

Fartown – Huddersfield's county ground – was the traditional venue for Huddersfield League set-piece occasions. This was the case for the 1948 Sykes Cup final. The Pack Horse Hotel was evidently keen to publicise its services. The Sykes Cup final was, after all, a major civic occasion, with large numbers of dignitaries and local cricket enthusiasts in attendance.

Lascelles Hall in July 1951 – the opening delivery of the Sykes Cup semi-final against Rastrick.

The Lascelles Hall XIII (including scorer) pictured at Fartown in August 1961.

1825 - 1975 Celebration Match

Lascelles Hall

v

Yorkshire

Official Programme Thursday July 10   15p

Sponsored by Hill's Surplus Ltd.
Liversedge

Lascelles Hall Cricket Club

Established 1825

MEMBERS OF THE HUDDERSFIELD
CRICKET LEAGUE, SECTION 'A'

SEASON 1981
MEMBER'S CARD

Printed by Swiftprint, Huddersfield

A special 150th anniversary fixture (1975) and a member's card (1981).

54

Top: 1986 Sykes Cup final programme. Bottom left: Alec Lodge – club historian and long-serving Huddersfield League administrator.
Bottom right: Lascelles Hall win the 2004 Sykes Cup final.

CHAPTER 7
UPPER COLNE VALLEY: PENNINE COUNTRY

The Upper Colne Valley is a very distinctive area, dominated by factories, mills and attractive rural landscapes. It is a district that has a very special sense of its own identity and traditions. There is a Colne Valley Museum, a Colne Valley Male Voice Choir, and once upon a time there was a Colne Valley Cricket League too. The three major communities are set in archetypal Pennine country: Marsden, the closest to Lancashire and famous for its Luddite heritage; Slaithwaite, famous for its 'moonraking' tradition; and Linthwaite, still home to two Huddersfield League cricket teams (Linthwaite, Broad Oak), and once home to a third (Linthwaite Hall).

CRICKET.

SATURDAY'S MATCHES.
MARSDEN v. LASCELLES HALL.

The committee of the Marsden M.I.C.C. have been very active of late superintending the formation of a new ground for the club. They opened it on Saturday, pitting a team of eighteen local players against twelve of Lascelles Hall. The weather was nearly all that could be desired, but the ground was very dead, as owing to the severe frost of the winter the turfing was not completed until six weeks ago. W. Haigh, the captain of the district team, won the toss, and elected to bat. W. Haigh and S. Haigh were the only batsmen who got into double figures, the former being somewhat lucky. The innings closed for 50 runs, a total which it was thought, would be easily wiped off by the "Lassil Olers" (that's how the spectators pronounced it), though they had

In 1879 Marsden Mechanics Institute CC – probably the forerunner of Marsden CC – moved to a new ground. They played Lascelles Hall in the first game at the new venue.

In 1936 Marsden's pavilion at Hemplow was gutted by fire.

56

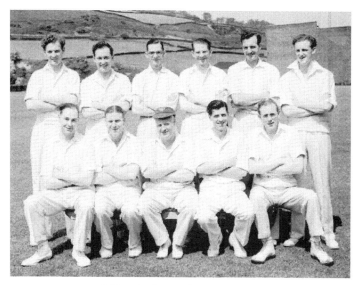

A Marsden line-up from May 1953.

D'OLIVEIRA OUTSTANDING
IN WHIT GAMES

Three quick fifties and six wickets

OUTSTANDING among Huddersfield Cricket League feats during the Whitsuntide cricket matches, blessed by ideal weather conditions, were those of the coloured South African player, Basil D'Oliveira, who deputised for Marsden professional, Pat Illingworth, on Monday and Tuesday.

Illingworth was playing for the Yorkshire second eleven against Lancashire II.

Playing at Linthwaite on Monday, D'Oliveira hit a magnificent 101, including thirty off one over, —the third individual century 30 for this season—and followed by capturing six Linthwaite wickets for 26 runs in seventeen overs as Linthwaite were dismissed for 70 runs.

On Tuesday at Marsden he captured only two wickets but going in at the fall of the first Marsden wicket promptly proceeded to hit 62, including two sixes and ten fours.

D'Oliveira scored his first fifty at Linthwaite in thirty-six minutes, his second in thirty-four minutes and the one at Marsden in thirty-two minutes.

As he is a professional he does not qualify for the quickest fifty ...

Association side lose at Barnsley

ALTHOUGH runs were scarce in the annual Whitsuntide match between Huddersfield and District Cricket Association and a Barnsley and District League XI at Grimethorpe Institute ground there was ample compensation for the crowd in the shape of some first rate bowling, backed up by excellent fielding.

Barnsley won their second game since the event was revived seven years ago in impressive fashion with six wickets in hand Huddersfield won the toss, elected to bat on what appeared to be a wicket full of runs, but surprisingly their batsmen were always struggling. Only two players, G. Taylor (18) and T. Wilkerson (12), reached double figures in the total of 74.

Of the Barnsley bowlers, D. Brown took four for 35 (in thirteen overs, two of which were maidens) and J. Carr four for 25 (in nine overs, three of which were maidens). The other successful bowlers were D. Mirfin (1—8) and T. Holding (1—5).

Barnsley got off to a tasky start, losing their opening pair, C. Brookes and J. Carr, for a meagre 19 runs. Both players fell victims to pace bowler D. Carter. Barnsley suffered a further shock when F. Berry brought off a fine one-handed catch to dismiss J. Tyne. The Barnsley ...

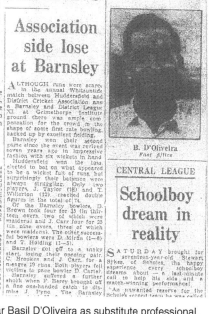

Whits

B. D'Oliveira
Fast fifties

CENTRAL LEAGUE

Schoolboy dream in reality

SATURDAY brought for seventeen-year-old Stewart Sykes of Scholes, the happy experience every schoolboy dreams about — a last-minute call to help his side, and a match-winning performance.

'An unwanted reserve for the Scholes second team he was called ...

In 1960 Marsden signed England Test star Basil D'Oliveira as substitute professional.

57

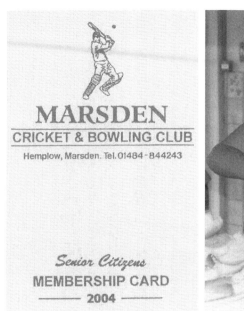

MARSDEN
CRICKET & BOWLING CLUB
Hemplow, Marsden. Tel. 01484-844243

Senior Citizens
MEMBERSHIP CARD
——— 2004 ———

Left: The club's 2004 fixture card. Right: A very enthusiastic Marsden tea lady.

In 1924 Slaithwaite CC scooped the Sykes Cup and Paddock Shield.

58

In 1933 the great West Indian Test cricketer Learie Constantine visited Slaithwaite.

Constantine meets the locals.

Above: Constantine's compatriot Edwin St. Hill signs for Slaithwaite at a fee of £240 (taken from a club scrapbook).

Hill Top, Slaithwaite in 1951

Star Slaithwaite stumper George Dawson.

SLAITHWAITE CRICKET & BOWLING CLUB - CRICKET FIXTURES SEASON 2004

DATE	1st XI	VENUE	DATE	2nd XI	VENUE
Sat April 17	Holmfirth	A	Sat April 17	HOLMFIRTH	H
Sun April 18	Buttershaw St Pauls		Sun April 18	B/E	
Sat April 24	ALMONBURY	H	Sat April 24	Almonbury	A
Sat May 01	Free Date		Sat May 01	Free Date	
Sun May 02	OLD ALMONDBURIANS	H	Sun May 02	Holmfirth	A
Sat May 08	Thongsbridge	A	Sat May 08	THONGSBRIDGE	H
Sun May 09	Kexborough	A	Sun May 09	KEXBOROUGH	H
Sat May 15	PADDOCK	H	Sat May 15	Paddock	A
Sat May 22	BROAD OAK	H	Sat May 22	Kirkburton	A
Sat May 29	Primrose Hill	A	Sat May 29	PRIMROSE	H
Mon May 31	Golcar	A	Mon May 31	GOLCAR	H
Sat June 05	ARMITAGE BRIDGE	H	Sat June 05	Clayton West	A
Sat June 12	Holmfirth	A	Sat June 12	HOLMFIRTH	H
Sat June 19	RASTRICK	H	Sat June 19	Rastrick	A
Sat June 26	Emley Clarence	A	Sat June 26	EMLEY CLARENCE	H
Sat July 03	Kirkheaton	A	Sat July 03	KIRKHEATON	H
Sat July 10	Lepton Highlanders	A	Sat July 10	LEPTON H'LANDERS	H
Sat July 17	PRIMROSE HILL	H	Sat July 17	Primrose Hill	A
Sat July 24	GOLCAR	H	Sat July 24	Golcar	A
Sat July 31	Armitage Bridge	A	Sat July 31	CLAYTON WEST	H
Sat Aug 07	MARSDEN	H	Sat Aug 07	Marsden	A
Sat Aug 14	Almondbury	A	Sat Aug 14	ALMONDBURY	H
Sat Aug 21	HOLMFIRTH	H	Sat Aug 21	Holmfirth	A
Sat Aug 28	Free Date		Sat Aug 28	Free Date	
Sun Aug 29	THONGSBRIDGE	H	Sun Aug 29	Thongsbridge	A
Sat Sept 04	KEXBOROUGH	H	Sat Sept 04	Kexborough	A
Sun Sept 05	Paddock	A	Sun Sept 05	PADDOCK	H
Sat Sept 11	Broad Oak	A	Sat Sept 11	KIRKBURTON	H

Sykes Cup & Paddock Shield
2nd Round - 23rd May
3rd Round - 20th June
Semi-Finals 4th, 11th & 18th July
Sykes Cup Final - 8th August
Paddock Shield Final - 15th August

Heavy Woollen Cup & Crowther Cup
2nd Rnd - 16th May 3rd Rnd 13th June
4th Round - 27th June
Semi-Finals - 18th July
Heavy Woollen Cup Final - 1st August
Crowther Cup Final - 30th August

Mini Cricket - 11th May - 8th June - 3rd August - Grand Finals Day - 12th Sept

Inter-Conference Play-Off Finals - 18th Sept

The club's 2004 fixture card.

WESTWOOD UNITED CRICKET CLUB.
Winners of the Colne and Holme Valley League, 1905-6-7.

Another Colne Valley side from yesteryear.

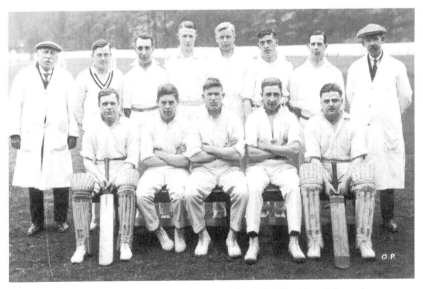

Linthwaite CC in 1929 – complete with distinguished-looking club umpires

LINTHWAITE

Thrice Champions Of The Huddersfield League

When the *Huddersfield Examiner* launched a special series on the history of local cricket clubs, the Linthwaite club were singled out for lavish praise.

The Linthwaite players come out at Fartown for the 1950 Sykes Cup final.

Membership tickets from the 1970s.

From little acorns...

The other club in the village are Broad Oak, who reached 100 not out in 1980.

64

Broad Oak's new clubhouse was officially opened by W. Beaumont Esq. on 18 December 1937.

Left: Harry Hinchliffe captured 1,000 Huddersfield League wickets for the club between 1934 and 1947 – a unique feat.
Right: J. Washington scored a record 210 in the Sykes Cup semi-final of 1928.

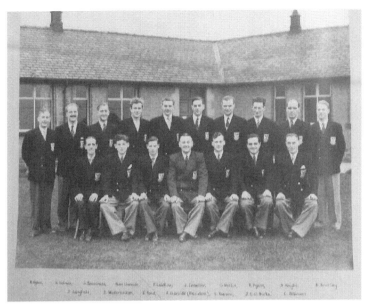

An official Broad Oak club photo from 1953.

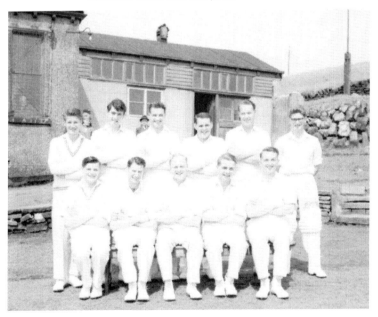

A team line-up from July 1960.

66

CHAPTER 8
LOWER HOLME VALLEY: HONLEY AND SURROUNDS

The Lower Holme Valley centres on Honley, a quintessentially English village. Towards Huddersfield you also encounter the villages of Armitage Bridge and Lockwood; towards Holmfirth, Thurstonland and Thongsbridge. In fact, two of the oldest clubs in the area are situated here – Armitage Bridge (1839) and Honley (c.1846).

Honley Wesleyans had a shortlived existence. This photograph records the opening of their new ground at Grasscroft on 24 May 1902. Their first fixture pitted them against Honley Congregationals.

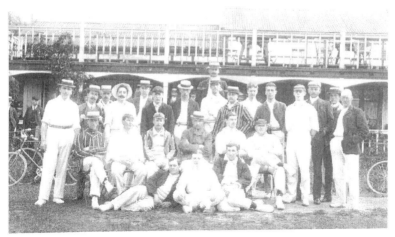

Honley were always the major club in the village. This is an early team photo from 1890.

A wartime club document.

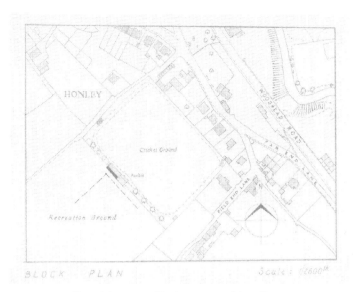

The cricket ground in the context of the village.

At last! Honley claim the Sykes Cup for the first time in 1982.

Left: Established in 1839, Armitage Bridge are one of the oldest clubs in the area. This is their club crest. Right: In 1938 club member Jack Crum achieved the amazing feat of throwing a cricket ball over the nearby Lockwood Viaduct.

An old aerial view of the club's ground, Armitage Fold.

ARMITAGE BRIDGE CRICKET CLUB

CRICKET MATCH

ARMITAGE BRIDGE C.C.
v
SIR LEONARD HUTTON'S X1

on Sunday, 2nd September, 1973
Wickets Pitched 2-0 pm

On the Occasion of the opening of the New Clubhouse

Bar, Refreshments & Stalls   **Tickets 10p**

THE MOORHOUSES, of Armitage Bridge Cricket Club, are century-makers. They can claim that their association is likely to cover 100 years.

Four generations have played with the club and three are still living.

Mr Abraham Moorhouse, aged eighty-one, who lives at 8, Calder Drive, Berry Brow, recalls that his father, George, who died in 1928, at seventy-four, was knocking a ball around at the club when he was quite a nipper, and played at the age of thirteen.

George's brothers, Bob and Fred, were county players. Bob

was a Yorkshire batsman and Fred played with Warwickshire.

Abraham, who retired as a civil servant sixteen years ago, played for Armitage Bridge until he was fifty and is a vice-president.

His brother, Harry, who lives at Waterloo, also played for Armitage Bridge.

Abraham's son, Roy, aged forty-two, of 6, Wain Park, Berry Brow, was secretary of the club for six years until last year and has been on the committee for twenty years.

His son, sixteen-year-old Robert, plays for the juniors and occasionally for the second team.

Above left: Len Hutton visit in 1973.
Above right: The famous Moorhouse family of Armitage Bridge.
Below: The club's 150th anniversary in 1989 – 'President's Lunch' featuring club president Ralph Beaumont.

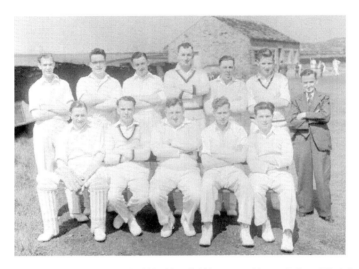

Lockwood CC were a distinguished Huddersfield League side, and played their home games only a few hundred yards away from Armitage Bridge's ground. The team picture comes from May 1953; the view of the ground, April 1953. Lockwood eventually merged with Huddersfield CC in 1991, and that club folded in 2002.

The foundation stone at Woodfield Park – home to the Huddersfield Police cricket club – was laid in 1929, although the history of local police cricket teams goes back to the turn of the century.

The Borough Police XI – 1950.

THURSTONLAND C. C.

This village has the reputation of having turned out some real sterling cricketers in the past, and once again the Club has shown its old love for the game by arranging a good list of fixtures. Most of the local clubs are met, and in the local Cup Ties the team will meet Netherthong, on their own ground. With ordinary luck the Club should have a good record at the close of the season.

May	7	Woodale, h
"	14	Hoyland Swaine, h
"	21	Cartworth Moor, a
"	28	Netherthong, a
June	11	Shelley, a
"	18	Scholes, h
"	25	Netherthong, cup tie, h
July	9	Wooldale, a
"	16	Scholes, a
"	23	Hoyland Swaine, a
"	30	Shelley, h
Aug.	6	Birdsedge, a
"	13	Birdsedge, h
"	20	Colne Bridge, h
"	27	Cartworth Moor, h
Sept.	3	Netherthong, h
"	17	Colne Bridge, a

Above: A Thurstonland CC fixture list from 1892.
Below: An early Thurstonland XII

Thurstonland Cricket Team—1906

Back Row:— B. Charlesworth, J. Hall, B. Kaye, S. Walker, G. Hirst.
Middle Row:— E. Gill, H. Pontefract, F. Lee, J. Lodge, W. H. Potter.
Front Row:— C. Mitchell, S. Fox.

74

Wesleyans fail to avoid drop

First title triumph for Thurstonland

THURSTONLAND clinched a Huddersfield Central League double and Upper Hopton took the Section "B" title as rain decimated the penultimate series of matches.

Allsop Cup winners Thurstonland took the Section "A" title for the first time after their home match against Hoylandswaine was washed out along with challengers Scholes' game at Denby Dale.

Thurstonland now go into Sunday's final match at Lepton an unassailable five points clear.

It's the same situation for Upper Hopton, who are six clear of second-placed Bradley and Colne, who are guaranteed promotion along with either Cumberworth or Holmbridge.

Almondbury Wesleyans will be the only team relegated from the top flight because of the departure of

Scholes and Penistone into the Huddersfield League.

Birchencliffe, Shelley, Bretton and Penistone Sports are fighting to avoid the one relegation place in Section "B."

Higham "B" boosted their Section "C" promotion hopes by completing their home match against relegated Woolley "B," who reached 110-9 as Newton bowled through and took seven for 42. Beevis hit an unbeaten 37 to give Higham a two-wicket win in the 31st over as White took six for 54.

Leymoor lead the section by one point from YMCA and both are ensured promotion. The third place will go to either Cartworth Moor or Higham "B," who

are three points behind. Leymoor entertain the Moor on Sunday, while Higham travel to YMCA.

SECTION "A"
Thurstonland v Hoylandswaine 11-2 in 8.3.
Denby Dale 13-6 v Scholes.
Emley v Denby 39-0 in 7.

SECTION "B"
Upper Hopton 30-1 in 11 v Cumberworth.
David Browns 58-1 in 16 v Bradley and Colne.
Bretton 21-2 in 12 v Penistone Sports.
Elockton 43-2 in 10 v Birchencliffe.

SECTION "C"
YMCA 58-2 in 25 v Upper Hopton "B."

HIGHAM "B" v WOOLLEY "B"

WOOLLEY "B"	
White c Gray b Newton	39
Brown c Shaw b Newton	11
Norton (D) lbw b Newton	1
Leishman c Shaw b Newton	0
Podolski b Gray	16
Norton (J) b Newton	9
Creswroft b Newton	12
Griffiths st Bamforth b Newton	0
Ward b Lockwood	9

Ogley not out	2
What not out	0
Extras	11
45 overs Total (for 9)	110

James 0-26, Newton 7-42, Lockwood 1-16, Gray 1-19.

HIGHAM "B"	
Shaw lbw b Norton (D)	26
Shawley b White	1
Lockwood c Ogley b White	15
James st Brown b White	2
Gray lbw b White	0
Askew run out	2
Beevis not out	37
Newton (K) c Brown b White	9
Wroe b White	4
Bamforth not out	0
Extras	9
Total (for 8)	113

Norton (D) 1-52, White 6-54.
Higham "B" 3pts Woolley "B" 1pt.

Bradford League

BRIGHOUSE v CLECKHEATON

BRIGHOUSE	
Jameson c Brook b Tighe	13
Rayner c Horkin b Tighe	1
Nichols b Tighe	13
Creswell lbw b Scansfield	10

VAUXHALL

X REG VAUXHALL ASTRA ESTATE. IN WHITE WITH DARK ORANGE UPHOLSTERED SEATING. MATCHING FITTED CARPETS. HEATED REAR WINDOW, REAR WASH WIPE AND ALL 1500 S REFINEMENTS. VERY, VERY NICE CONDITION AND LOW MILEAGE.

In 1987 Thurstonland claimed a Central League double.

In 2005 Thurstonland were the subject of a special BBC Radio 4 *Open Country* documentary on village cricket.

75

Joyce Booth is one of the most prominent women in the local cricket world. She is a stalwart of the Thurstonland club – and was also made a Vice-President of the Huddersfield Central League.

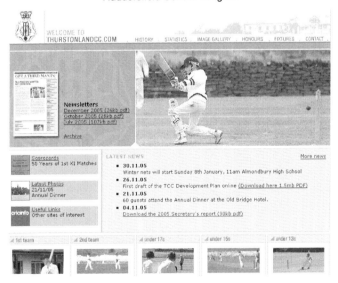

Thurstonland CC also boast an excellent website.

Thongsbridge Cricket Team, 1910.

Winners of the Lumb Cup and Association Cup.
Back Row : L. Greenwood, W. MacLintock, W. Jessop, A. Lancaster, J. Hudson.
Second Row : D. Beaumont, A. Bottomley, C. Haigh (Capt.), A. Beaumont, H. Sanderson.
Front Row : N. Beaumont (Lumb Cup), T. L. Buchanan (Association Cup), C. Bottomley.

The Thongsbridge 'Double'-winning side of 1910.

The 1950 women's tea committee.

Left: Publicity for the club's 1960 Annual Dinner.
Right: Club stalwart Jim Dawson who also served the Huddersfield League with distinction.

A flooded Miry Lane ground – 1972.

CHAPTER 9
UPPER HOLME VALLEY: PICTURE POSTCARD LAND

The Upper Holme Valley is one of the most picturesque parts of South Kirklees. Holmfirth is its centre – as a town, famous for *Last of the Summer Wine*, the manufacture of picture postcards, and second-hand bookshops – but Meltham to the north-west is also a sizeable community. The surrounding villages are beautiful and also passionate about their cricket: Holmbridge, Cartworth Moor, Scholes and Upperthong.

There were so many factories and mills in the area that early in the last century a special cricket competition was established to cater for works teams. In 1919 Digley Mills were the local champions.

These 11 men took Holmfirth to local cricketing glory in 1867. The variety of garments on display indicates that this is very much the pre-'whites' era. In this period, the type of headwear being worn often denoted socio-economic background and class.

CRICKET.

The first match of importance played since the opening of this year's cricket season took place on Saturday at Holmfirth. The weather was delightfully fine, but bitterly cold. The attendance, particularly in the afternoon, was extremely good. It could hardly be said that the United North were well represented, as several well-known performers were absentees. With George Pinder, Armitage, Albert Champion, J. Ulyett and A. Greenwood, however, they were by no means weak, especially considering that they were supported by several gentlemen bats. The twenty two won the toss and went in first, Champion and Mr. Kilner undertaking the bowling. The former, who this season goes to Longsight, Manchester, as professional, was in rare form, while Pinder, behind the stumps, performed in very good style. No particularly important stand was made by any of the batsmen except J. Thewlis, jun., who put 24 together by steady play, combined with hard hitting when the opportunity came. Two remarkably fine catches were made in the long-field by Andrew Greenwood, another by Mr. W. R. Wake, and another by Armitage, who had to run a long way with the sun in his eyes. The innings closed for a total of 83. The Eleven sent in Mr. W. R. Wake and Mr. Kilner, and two wickets were down without a run. Andrew Greenwood made a stand, but no one else did much, and the innings closed for 43, the Twenty-two thus winning easily. Score:—

TWENTY-TWO.		THE ELEVEN.	
G. W. Walker, b Champion	0	Mr. W. R. Wake, st Quarmby b Littlewood	0
J. Littlewood, c Barrows b Ellis	14	Mr. S. Ellis, b Littlewood	0
K. H. Hardy, st Pinder b Champion	1	Mr. S. Shaw, b Littlewood	2
Wm. Kaye, c Barrows b Ellis	8	A. Champion, c A. H ap b Kaye	1
C. W. Longbottom, c Armitage b Ulyett	3	A. Greenwood, c Coldwell b Dawson	15
J. W. Heap, b Ellis	5	J. Ulyett, c B. Little - ood	
A. Heap, lbw b Champion	8	b J. Littlewood	5
J. Thewlis, b Pinder	24	G. Pinder, c Quarmby b Kaye	8
J. Healey, b Champion	1	T. Armitage, b Kaye	0
J. Brook, c Greenwood b Champion	1	— Barrows, not out	4
W. Coldwell, c Greenwood b Champion	0	— Eastwood, b Kaye	0
T. W. Quarmby, b Champion	4		
R. Littlewood, c ast b Ulyett	1		
J. B. Coldwell, c Greenwood b Ulyett	3		
J. Dawson, b Ulyett	0		
J. Wilkinson, c Wake b Pinder			
H. Beal, b Ulyett			
F. M Nish, c S. Shaw b Pinder	2		
R. M Nish, b Barrows	2		
W. Healey, not out	3		
H. Frampton, c Eastwood b Pinder	0		
C. Coldwell, run out	0		
Total	83	Total	43

In this early period, professional touring sides often played 'odds' matches against local teams. When Holmfirth played the United North in 1880 they fielded 22 men to make the contest an even one.

Huddersfield League champions in the late-1890s.

Graffiti plague
at cricket club

(From page 1)
broken; pavilion windows smashed; bottles and barrels smashed. It cannot surely be a excuse that young people have nothing else to do, with the Sands site having been developed. It is a sad state of affairs when young people resort to this sort of behaviour for amusement."

Officials have remonstrated with groups of teenagers, but have faced a torrent of abuse.

"We know it is only a minority of young people — most are courteous and helpful — but these mindless few are ruining facilities for everyone else," said Mr

Like many local cricket clubs, Holmfirth have suffered the plague of vandalism. This cutting comes from February 2002.

A plan of Meltham's ground in 1923.

Meltham's A. Topp, J. Barker and G. Dawson in 1952.

Action from Meltham's 1962 Sykes Cup semi-final against Paddock.

In 1973 Test spinner Dilip Doshi won the Huddersfield League bowling prize while playing for Meltham. This photo of the Indian star now hangs in the new Mean Lane clubhouse.

Over the years Meltham has been a cricketing hotspot. Above: Meltham Mills CC - Byrom Shield winners - in 1898. Below: Helme CC, winners of the Lumb Cup in 1911.

HOLME BRIDGE BRITTANNIA *v.* LITTLE HAYFIELD.—
This match was played on Saturday last, on the
ground of the former, and resulted in an easy victory
for them. Score :—

Britannia. — B. A. Haigh 16, A. P. Mellor 23, G. H.
Marsden 2, W. Booth 3, R. Biltcliffe 12, J. Booth 18,
L. Kaye 8, J. A. Brook 0, M. Bailey 4, C. Booth 11, F.
Dawson not out 0, extras 21 ; total 118.

Little Hayfield. —Jno. Bradley 0, E. Cooper 0, G.
Tomlinson 1, Joseph Bradley 0, C. Parker 2, T. Leach
3, C. Hadfield 3, J. R. Wardle 0, J. Hyam 0, J. Hobson
0, W. Bradley not out 1, extras 2 ; total 12.

Holmbridge is a delightful village south of Holmfirth. Holme Bridge Britannia were an early
incarnation of Holmbridge Cricket Club. Their opposition in this 1871 match – Little
Hayfield – indicates that the village looked to rural Derbyshire for some of their fixtures in
the pre-league era.

This was the Holmbridge side that claimed the Huddersfield Central League championship
in 1931.

Holmbridge was also a hotbed of women's cricket.

Yorkshire and England star Len Hutton visited the club in 1956 to present the end-of-season prizes.

CARTWORTH MOOR C. C.

This club continues to show signs of improvement in its constitution. The bazaar has placed it on a very sound and satisfactory foundation, so that the club lacks no material support with a prosperous future. The fixture list is quite as strong if not stronger than usual, and as will be seen the team has to meet Holmfirth 2nd in the Cup Ties. Holmfirth Tradesmen also visit the club's ground.

May 7 Scholes, a
„ 14 Wooldale, a
„ 21 Thurstonland, h
„ 28 Birdsedge, h
June 4 Shepley, a
„ 6 Midhope, a
„ 7 Holmfirth Tradesmen, h
„ 11 Midhope, h
„ 18 Holmfirth 2nd, Cup Tie a
„ 25 Lindley Parish Church, h
July 2 Clayton West a
„ 16 Lindley Parish Church, a
„ 23 Clayton West, h
„ 30 Netherthong, h
Aug. 6 Shepley, h
„ 13 Scholes, h
„ 20 Birdsedge, a
„ 27 Thurstonland, a
Sept 3 Wooldale, h
„ 10 Netherthong, a
„ 17 Holmfirth 2nd, a

Cartworth Moor's ground on Gill Lane is one of the highest in Yorkshire, if not England. This early fixture list shows that the club rarely played teams from outside the Holmfirth/Denby Dale area – the exception here being Lindley Parish Church. Like many other clubs, Moor also held fundraising bazaars, and they were clearly very successful.

The Cartworth Moor team in 1905.

1934 Holden Cup winners – the cricketers in white are outnumbered by proud club members in suits!

Mountain of molehills undermines grant bid

By DAVID EYRE

HOLME Valley Parish Council has refused to give a grant to a local cricket club — because of a mountain of molehills.

Cartworth Moor Cricket Club had applied for help with the reseeding and levelling of their pitch.

But at last week's finance committee meeting councillors decided not to give any money to the club until they were sure a long-running battle with the moles was won.

The animals have been leaving large molehills all over the pitch.

Clr Donald Firth told the meeting that he had problems with moles this summer himself, and wanted some kind of guarantee that club would get rid of them before a grant was made.

He said: "If we give the club a grant, how de we know the moles won't return to destroy the newly-laid pitch? We can't make sure they've gone away."

Clr Keith Horn said he was disappointed that the club was not going to get a grant, as it was the only institution in Cartworth to get any money from the parish council, but he agreed with Clr Firth on the mole issue.

"If they come back and say they've got rid of the moles then we'll look at it again," he said.

Former Kirklees Mayor Ken Sims also told the committee that the funds for last year's Mayor's appeal for Breast Cancer Research, were closed. About £17,000 had been raised for the charity.

In August 1996 the club encountered a serious mole problem.

Scholes CC are very proud of their history, and their birth date in 1876.

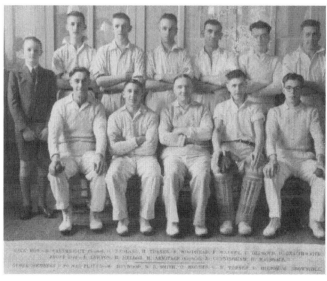

Scholes were Huddersfield Central League champions in 1943. The cricketers were smartly attired – as was the scorer too!

The 1962 Scholes CC Annual Dinner was held at Dunford Bridge.

No Council sale of cricket land to Scholes club

SCHOLES Cricket Club's attempts to buy their ground were hit for six by Holmfirth General Purposes Committee last night.

The Clerk to the Council, Mr. D. H. Nicholson, pointed out that a small portion of land near the field had been given to the Council and was used by the club. "The Council could sell the larger piece of ground to the club if it wanted but would then be left with the smaller part," said Mr. Nicholson.

He added: "Consequently if Scholes Cricket Club goes out of existence and we had sold them the land, they would be able to resell it and we would be left with a useless little piece of land.

"Village cricket is losing popularity and there is a danger of these clubs going out of existence."

Mr. Nicholson's suggestion that it would be better not to sell was moved by Clr. E. B. Kaye and accepted by the committee.

The Council will be recommended to ask the local Sports Development Council to find out the financial requirements of all Holmfirth and district's sporting associations. This follows an application by the Holmfirth Parish Church Tennis Club for a grant.

In 1971 Scholes were barred from buying their own ground by the local council. But note the council view that: 'Village cricket is losing popularity and there is a danger of these clubs going out of existence.' In the twenty-first century Scholes CC continues to thrive!

Upperthong are a relatively young cricket club. Cricket had been played in the village since 1977 but UCC only joined the Huddersfield Central League in 1999 – and claimed Central League silverware in 2000.

Upperthong play high up above Holmfirth, and visiting players enter the clubhouse through this door.

CHAPTER 10
DENBY DALE AND DISTRICT: PIES AND PAVILIONS

Denby Dale – 'The Pie Village' – is also home to a cricket club that has reinvented itself in recent years thanks to a new pavilion. The Pie Hall is situated only yards away from the cricket club, and it is a toss-up as to which is the most significant institution in the village. Down one road is Denby – a very distinct settlement from Denby Dale. Down another is Cumberworth – home to the legendary Friend Allsop and a second state-of-the-art clubhouse.

Denby Dale are a club that in recent times have benefited from the availability of lottery funding. The award of a £200,000 grant in 1997 enabled the club to attract finance from other sources and build a modern pavilion, which also incorporates business space. It was opened in 1999 with a match against the England women's cricket team. The past was not forgotten at the dawn of this new era - and the new pavilion was named after Zachariah Hinchcliffe, a local mill owner who had been instrumental in the formation of the club towards the end of the nineteenth century.

CRICKET.

HUDDERSFIELD AND DISTRICT COMBINATION.

RESULTS UP TO DATE.

	Played.	Won.	Lost.	Drawn.	Pts.
Denby Dale	22	15	2	5	35
Scholes	22	11	4	7	29
Shelley	22	12	7	3	27
Netherthong	22	11	8	3	25
Helme	22	10	8	4	24
Cartworth Moor	22	8	8	6	22
Cumberworth United	22	7	8	7	21
St. Andrew's	22	7	10	5	19
Thurstonland	22	6	10	6	18
Lepton Highlanders	22	6	10	6	18
Crosland Moor	22	5	13	4	14
Colnebridge	22	4	12	6	14

JOHN BROOK, Hon. Sec.

Top of the tree in 1897!

An undated photograph of Dale players walking out to the middle.

Taking a look at the devastation are, from left: former player Mr S Simpson, groundsman/player Mr B Cocking, player Mr P Senior and his son Jonathan (8)

An unusual feature of Denby Dale's picturesque Wakefield Road ground is the stream that runs underneath the square. During the 1920s work was carried out to cover the watercourse with a concrete raft which was supported by railway sleepers. During heavy flooding in 1982 some of the railway sleepers collapsed, leaving a series of holes in the pitch.

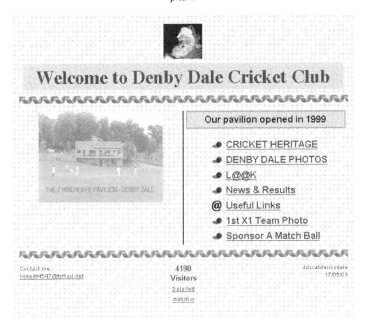

Like some other clubs, DDCC have an impressive website facility.

94

CRAIK's v. DENBY UNITED. — At Denby. Score:

.DENBY.			CRAIK'S.	
Waddie b Penty	3		Firth b Wood	6
Wood b Guest	5		Gibson b Wood	16
Dransfield c Fozzard b			Newton b Wood	0
Pollitt	5		Chappell b Wood	0
Shirt b Guest	4		Whittle b Wood	2
Woodhead b Guest	1		Pollitt b Wood	0
Gaunt b Guest	3		Guest c Barraclough b	
Womersley run out	1		Gaunt	0
J. Gaunt b Pollitt	6		Brown b Wood	12
Barraclough not out	2		Fozzard c Womersley b	
Gibson c Newton b			Gaunt	5
Pollitt	0		Sykes c & b Wood	0
Turton b Sykes	2		Penty not out	1
Extras	5		Extras	6
Total	37		Total	48

There is some confusion about the origins of Denby Cricket Club, but around the turn of the twentieth century, a team called Denby United were fulfilling fixtures, like this one in 1901. The 'United' might have signified the merger of two teams in the village – or a coming together of the communities of Upper and Lower Denby to form a sporting organisation. In later years, the club would also, occasionally, be referred to as 'Upper Denby' on account of its geographical location.

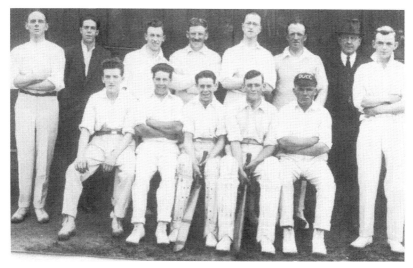

A team photo from 1932 – note the customised DUCC caps.

Secretary. C. Crosland. Treasurer. J. Gaunt.
Interest waning, efforts to field
a team each week for Penistone
League matthermade but occasionally
the team had to field only ten
men.

Captain. F. Burdett.
V. Captain. P. Lodge.

Members. P. Lodge. F. Burdett. O. Marsh.
A. Lockwood. M. Lockwood. R. Swift.
P. Beever. A. Holmes. T. Lamsdon.
D. Knowles. W. Knowles. W. Martin.
J. Wright.

Minutes from the 1957 AGM. In 1958 the club went into hibernation for a couple of years due to lack of players.

SOUTH YORKSHIRE LEAGUE.
Brampton 33, Bolton 41 (for 3).
Rawmarsh 105, Darfield 111 (for 7).
PENISTONE & DISTRICT LEAGUE
(Division 1).
Penistone Church 86, Thurgoland 78.
Crane Moor 51, Hoylandswaine 27.
Denby 73, Silkstone United 77 (for 7).
(Division 2.)
Thurgoland 28, Penistone Church 34 (for 4).
Thurlstone Wesleyans 21, Stocksbridge Old 34 (for 4).
"TINKER" CUP.—SEMI-FINAL.
Penistone Netherfield 150, Clayton West 74.
Cumberworth 162, Penistone Y.S. & I.W. 38.

Historically, Denby is part of the Parish of Penistone, and the cricket club played in the Penistone & District League until it switched to the Huddersfield Central League in 1961.

Left: A fixture card from 1967. The club are proud to say they are members of the Huddersfield Central League. Right: Joining the new league meant that, after over half a century of playing matches elsewhere, the focus moved to the Huddersfield area. In 1979 David Firth and Howard Moxon prepared to open the batting at Thurstonland.

14 ; total 53.

KIRKBURTON. -D. Hoyle 7, R. Carter 4, J. Hoyle 0, Garner 0, Womersley 3, Dyson 6, S. Carter 1, Binns 0, A. Carter 1, Earnshaw (not out) 1, Hill 0, extras 4 ; total 27.

THURSTONLAND v. CUMBERWORTH.—Played at Cumberworth, on Saturday last. The home team won easily. Score :—

THURSTONLAND.—Walton 2, Lodge 1, Thewlis 8, Heywood 8, Kaye 0, Booth 3, Walker 0, Hadfield 3, Firth 1, Heywood (not out) 0, Chadwick 0, extras 19 ; total 45.

CUMBERWORTH.—Peace 0, Riding 2, W. H. Hirst 6, Haigh 10, Biltcliffe 0, Wilkinson 9, Smith 4, Jepson 1, Seth Cook 6, J. Cook (not out) 1, J. Hirst 9 ; extras 14 ; total 62.

SKELMANTHORPE v. EMLEY.—Played at Skelmanthorpe on Saturday last. Score :—

SKELMANTHORPE.—Tarbett 0, H. Kilner 18, Robinson 6, Field 0, Cockroft 0, Jepson (not out) 11, Fisher 1, W. Ellis 2. J. Ellis 0. R. Kilner 0. Biltcliffe 3. extras

Left: One of Cumberworth's earliest fixtures came in 1876 – a local derby against Thurstonland. Right: Friend Allsop was a legendary figure on the local cricket scene – a true sportsman in every sense. After his death, Cumberworth donated the 'Allsop Cup' to the Huddersfield Central League in memory of his services to cricket. The Allsop Cup became the 1st XI knockout cup and is still played for today.

The Cumberworth United side that lined up against Nortonthorpe at Shelley in the Allsop Cup final of 1961.

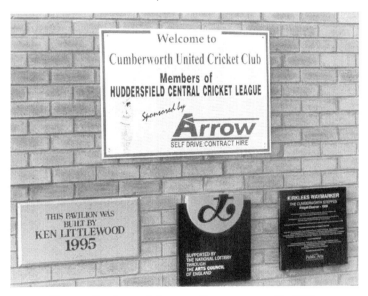

The new Cumberworth Lane pavilion was opened in 1995.

Members of Cumberworth Cricket Club discuss plans to turn a heap of debris into a work of art.

A public meeting is planned at Cumberworth First School on Friday at 7.45pm to discuss the plans to create the *Cumberworth Steppes* out of the spoil heap formed 100 years ago when the Cumberworth railway tunnel was created.

Pictured discussing the plans are Mr Philip Senior (left) secretary/treasurer of the club and Mr Nigel Senior (right), the club's chairman.

London artist Abigail Downer will discuss her plans to terrace the heap as the sixth in the series of 12 landmarks being created around the 72-mile circular Kirklees Walk.

The project is being carried out by Wakefield-based arts consultancy Public Arts in conjunction with a local group.

The spoil heap is alongside the cricket club's new £55,000 pavilion, built to replace one which burned down in August. The pavilion has been partly funded by a grant of more than £30,000 from the national lottery.

The club have also embraced culture and sculpture in recent years. The Cumberworth Steppes – in essence, a terraced area behind the pavilion where a railway tunnel was once sited – are now an integral part of the Kirklees Way.

Allsop Cup winners in 2001.

CHAPTER 11
DEARNE VALLEY: THE VILLAGE GAME

Lepton and Kirkburton are the gateway to the Dearne Valley, which comprises a constellation of small, handsome villages that almost define themselves by their cricket teams and the rivalry that has endured between them for a century and more: Shelley, Skelmanthorpe, Shepley, Nortonthorpe (Scissett) and Clayton West. Throw in a number of former clubs, such as Rowley Hill CC and Storthes Hall CC, and you have an area of great passion for the noble game.

This letter from 1873 shows that Lepton Highlanders CC were very keen to raise funds for the club.

This was one of Lepton's early successful sides. There are 20 people on this photograph –
players, officials and umpires - which shows that the title was viewed as a genuine club
triumph.

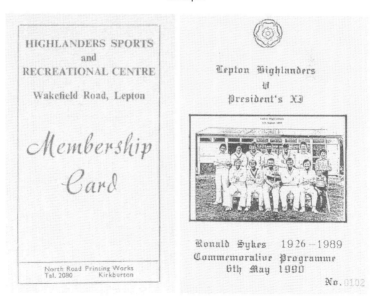

Left: This club documentation dates from 1978.
Right: This was the programme for a special event in 1990.

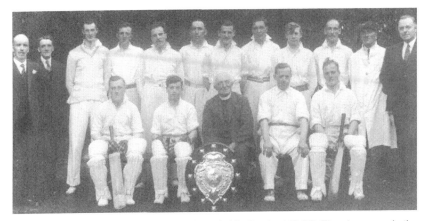

An undated team photograph of Lepton-based side Rowley Hill CC. The clergyman in the middle of the front row tells us that it was a church-based team.

KIRKBURTON V. KIRKHEATON.

On Saturday a match between these clubs was played on the Kirkheaton ground, and resulted in a win for Kirkburton by twenty seven runs. The fielding on both sides was very good, scarcely a chance being missed, and some unlikely ones (as that of Hargreaves by Lodge, &c., Stringer by Carter,) were taken. Wilson (left hand) bowled very well. The slows, though having little twist, were terribly destructive to the Kirkheaton team. The score ran thus :—

KIRKBURTON.

J. Sykes, run out	1
S. Carter, b Wilson	12
J. Brooke, b Wilson	15
B. Copley, b Wilson	5
A. Micklethwaite, b F. Thornton	6
L. Lodge, b Lodge	2
N. Haigh, c Rowbottom b Wilson	0
G. Roebuck, not out	7
W. Haigh, b Wilson	0
J. Charlesworth, b Lodge	1
C. Hargreaves, c Lodge b Wilson	0
Extras	12
Total	60

KIRKHEATON.

M. Hill, b Micklethwaite	1
J. Rowbottom, st Copley b Brooke	0
D. Stringer, c Carter b Brooke	2
W. Lodge, run out	7
D. Hey, c Micklethwaite b Brooke	0
F. Thornton, b Brooke	0
J. Broadhead, c Charlesworth b Brooke	1
R. Grange, not out	5
S. Wilson, c Sykes b Brooke	9
J. H. Haley, b Brooke	0
J. Thornton, b Brooke	5
Extras	3
Total	33

This early fixture involving Kirkburton took place in 1867. 'Burton also came out on top!

These were the 'Boys of 1904' – the 12 cricketers who took Kirkburton to Alliance League success in that year. Key club officials are also sharing in the success.

This bus served as a makeshift pavilion while the new clubhouse was built in 1960/1.

In 1998 England Test all-rounder Phil Defreitas helped Kirkburton out when they were short of a professional. Here he is mingling with his new teammates.

In May 1954 a new cricket pavilion was opened at Storthes Hall, a hospital sited near Kirkburton.

This is the earliest photograph of Shelley cricketers – taken some time in the late nineteenth century. In this period, most of a village side's players would actually live in the village.

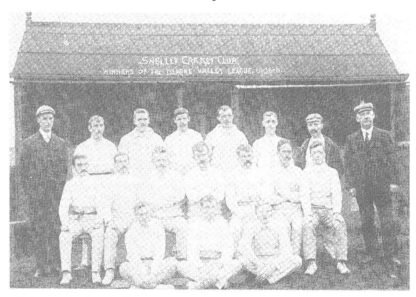

Before moving into the Huddersfield Central League, and then Huddersfield League, Shelley competed in the local Dearne Valley League, claiming the championship in 1905-6.

The Shelley XI that bagged the Allsop Cup in 1960.

Century Plus

THE SHELLEY CRICKET CLUB STORY 1871-1988

—BOB HAIGH

In 1988 club stalwart Bob Haigh compiled this excellent illustrated account of Shelley's history. The old pavilion adorned the front cover.

106

SKELMANTHORPE
CRICKET CLUB.

List of Officers, 1931.

President - C. E. FIELD, Esq.

Vice Presidents—

Mrs. C. E. Field,	F. Warren, Esq.	V. Hinchcliff, Esq.
Rev. R. Teale,	H. Dyson, Esq.	R. Heaton, Esq.
Sir P. H. Jackson,	J. Auckland, Esq.	R. J. Lawton, Esq.
J. T. Field, Esq.	W. Rothery, Esq.	G. T. Haigh, Esq.
F. E. Field, Esq.	H. S. Jackson, Esq.	F. Senior, Esq.
P. G. Field, Esq.	A. Cartwright, Esq.	H. Senior, Esq.
A. Dalton, Esq.	N. R. Micklethwaite, Esq.	

Patrons—

Dr. D. Bell	H. Mallows, Esq.	R. W. Naylor, Esq.
W. Hinchcliffe, Esq.	W. Naylorclty, Esq.	H. Curtridge, Esq.
H. Pogson, Esq.	R. Peel, Esq.	M. J. Taylor, Esq.
W. Dyson, Esq.	H. Dalton, Esq.	T. W. Tayton, Esq.
H. Flack, Esq.	S. Tyas, Esq.	

Secretary—C. Ellis.   *Treasurer—L. Dyson.*

League Representative. H. Freeman.

Skelmanthorpe CC played their first friendly fixtures in the 1870s. Half a century and more on, this was their roll-call of officials.

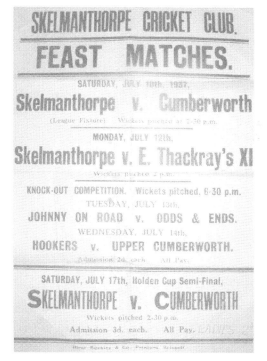

A club poster from 1937. Note the strange names of the teams taking part in the Feast games, and the fact that women were allowed in for 2d (an eleventh-hour decision?).

A presentation evening in the 1950s.

Females bowl 'em over at cricket club

By Karen Grattage

Women are leading the way into the new century at Skelmanthorpe Cricket Club — and they've caught positions as chair and vice-chair.

Margaret Dollive (left), a hospital worker, and Beverley Crossland (right), a local hairdresser, are the first female members of the committee and they've scooped top jobs.

Members say the club — which dates from the 1800's — is breaking new ground and it's all down to the ladies.

Women first became involved at Skelmanthorpe two years ago when a group of wives and mothers took on the role of renovating the club house.

Mrs Dollive said : "We did a lot of work behind the scenes doing fundraising and then painting and decorating the club.

"Everything was done — from putting up new curtains to refurbishing the bar. Now our main task is collecting money for new carpets."

Her first aim as chairman is to develop links between the junior and senior sides as well as open up the club to more women.

She said: "The ladies did have one match with the junior team last summer and we won with the help of a few strange tactics.

"My husband and sons have played for Skelmanthorpe but I first became involved when my dad was a cricketer, so it's always been part of my life."

Mrs Dollive and Mrs Crossland have already led two committee meetings and say they have been made very welcome.

Skelmanthorpe are probably unique in local league cricket circles in that they boast a female chairperson and vice-chairperson.

A champion Shepley side from 1900.

A Shepley club dinner during the 1950s.

The Marsh Laners reached 100 not out in 1971...

...and Indian Test legend Sunil Gavaskar visited Shepley in 1988.

NORTONTHORPE v. EMLEY (First Elevens.)—Played at Nortonthorpe, on Saturday last, resulting in an easy victory for the home team. The bowling of Littlewood, and the batting of T. Hudson, for Nortonthorpe, and the bowling of H. Blacker, for Emley, were particularly good. Score :—

EMLEY.—Stringer, c Buckley b Lockwood 0 ; Haigh, run out 0 ; Scargill, b Littlewood 0 ; J. Blacker, c G. H. Green b Littlewood 0 ; A. Wilkinson, b Littlewood 2, H. Blacker, b Littlewood 0 ; Swallow, b Littlewood 2 ; Gill, not out 4 ; Waltes, b Littlewood 0 ; G. Wilkinson, b Lockwood 1 ; Kaye, b Littlewood 0 ; extras 2 ; total 11.

NORTONTHORPE.—Hudson, b H. Blacker 7 ; Lockwood, c J. Blacker b H. Blacker 1 ; Cockcroft, b A. Wilkinson 1 ; Haigh, b A. Wilkinson 4 ; Turner, run out 3 ; Littlewood, b Swallow 3 ; Buckley, c A. Wilkinson b H. Blacker 0 ; Wilkinson, b H. Blacker 4 ; Dawson, not out 4 ; Green, b Swallow 0 ; Firth, b Swallow 1 ; extras 9 ; total 37.

NORTONTHORPE v. EMLEY.—Played at Emley, on Saturday last, resulting in an easy victory for the visitors. The batting of Green, Skinn, Clay, Hudson, and the bowling of Barker for Nortonthorpe, as also the bowling of Scargill for Emley, deserve special mention. Score :—

NORTONTHORPE.—Green 13, Barker 1, Wilkinson 4, Senior 1, Dyson 8, Hudson 11, Pewis 1, Walshaw 0, Skinn 11, Clay (not out) 10, Whitley 4, extras 5 ; total 74.

EMLEY.—Scargill 3, Booth 2, Scott 1, Pell 0, Haigh 7, Parker 0, Brook 8, Moxon 2, Beckett 0, Goward (not out) 1, Hirst 0, extras 3 ; total 26.

Nortonthorpe were playing fixtures against Emley in 1877.

BOB HAIGH takes a nostalgic look at the history of a local cricket club

Nortonthorpe's glory years

The local press have delved back into the club's rich history.

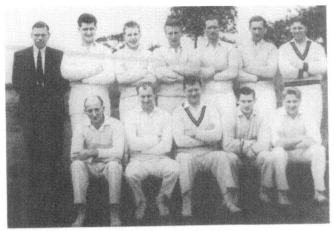

NORTONTHORPE C.C. 1963
STANDING: E. Monkman, N. Mosley, R. England, B. Glover, Dennis Bentley, M. Taylor, J. Battye
SEATED: F. Exley, S. Holden, R. Hardy (Capt.), K. Armitage, T. Kitson

The 1960s were the club's 'golden age'. They did the 1st XI 'Double' in 1963, and also won the 2nd XI Tinker Cup.

Roger Littlewood pictured at crisis club Nortonthorpe

Crisis club issues SOS

By Sally Simpson

A CALL has gone out to keen cricketers to come to the rescue of a local club in crisis.

Scissett-based Nortonthorpe Cricket Club, which rode high on a wave of success throughout the 1960s and '70s, is now

competition within the locality with a number of other clubs on our doorstep.

The club is financially solvent, but it is the playing strength that will be the deciding factor as to whether we can go on."

Dwindling team numbers forced the club to withdraw its second team from the Huddersfield

club raised the funds itself through the voluntary efforts of the people involved in the club.

"There are old stalwarts who would be turning in their graves if they could see the trouble the club is in now."

Formerly affiliated to Nortonthorpe Mills, the combined football and cricket club was sited on land held in trust for the Holme and Colne Valleys.

In 1999 Nortonthorpe hit difficult times but, thankfully, have survived.

112

	Played.	Won.	Lost.	Drwn.	Pts.
Shelley	18	12	2	4	28
Denby Dale	18	12	3	3	27
Nortonthorpe	18	11	4	3	26
Emley Clarence	18	6	6	6	18
Hepworth	18	6	8	4	16
Penistone	18	6	8	4	16
Clayton West	18	5	9	4	14
Shepley	18	5	9	4	14
Cumberworth	18	4	10	4	12
Cawthorne	18	2	10	6	10

Second Competition.

	Played.	Won.	Lost.	Drwn.	Pts.
Clayton West	18	14	2	2	30
Nortonthorpe	18	11	3	4	26
Cumberworth	18	11	4	3	25
*Cawthorne	18	7	7	4	17
Denby Dale	18	6	8	4	16
Emley Clarence	18	7	9	2	16
Shelley	18	5	8	5	15
Penistone	18	6	10	2	14
Shepley	18	5	10	3	13
Hepworth	18	2	13	3	7

*Cawthorne one point deducted for breach of rules.

W. HANSON, Secretary.

Clayton West were formed in the 1880s, and in 1906 claimed the Dearne Valley 2nd XI title.

A Clayton West line-up from July 1952.

Clayton West celebrated their 11th Huddersfield Central Cricket League Championship success at their annual dinner dance and prize presentation at the Springfield Park Hotel, Kirkburton. Skipper Adrian Whittaker (far right) is pictured with the Section A trophy with other prizewinners (from left): Stuart Rank, Ian Fisher (2nd XI captain) and Kevin Rank

1993 – The club's 11th Huddersfield Central League championship.

Clayton lift Premier title for 14th time

CLAYTON WEST have clinched the Yorkshire Electricity Huddersfield Central League's Premier Championship for the second time in three years, and with it, a League and Cup double.

Victory over Holmbridge and Hoylandswaine's defeat at Thurstonland assured Clayton of the title, and now makes next Sunday's top-of-the-table clash between Hoylandswaine and Clayton West irrelevant.

It was Clayton's 14th League Championship, and the second time they have achieved the double, but Mark England's side, who

CRICKET

Lockwood (G) b Brammall 0
Marsh c Oldham (D) b Brammall 17
Hardwick c Brammall b Denton 24
Burkinshaw b Brammall 12
Robinson not out 3
Beevor lbw b Rishton 8
Dickinson st Mason b Rishton 8
Storey not out 8
                         Extras 20

45 overs   Total (for 6) 80
Brammall 16-4-30-4, Peace 9-2-20-0,
Rishton 13-4-21-2, Denton 5-3-9-1
THURSTONLAND
Howarth lbw b Burkinshaw 8
Oldham (M) c and b Storey 8
Inglis lbw b Burkinshaw 1
Oldham (D) not out 39
Gloystaine c Marsh b Hoyle 1
Booth not out 24
                         Extras 14

36.4 overs   Total (for 4) 97
Burkinshaw 14-7-30-2, Storey 12-6-21,
Lockwood (D) 5-2-8-0, Hoyle 4-0-29-1,
Dickinson 1-0-6-0
Thurstonland 8pts Hoylandswaine 1pt

HIGHAM
James c Waring b Beresford 54
Osborne c Holt b Walker 4
Fearnley c Mahall b Walker 0
Horbury c Wimpenny (R) b
    Beresford 5
Heaton b Beresford 4
Smith st Ramsden (L) b Walker 5
Archer lbw b Beresford 4
Banks not out 23
Clayton run out 0
Abson b Walker 0
Bamforth not out 23
                        Extras 12

44.4 overs   Total (for 9) 143
Mahall 1-1-0, Waring 7-3-21-0, Walker
12-4-2-42-3, Beresford 14-1-28-4, Holt 7-1
16-0
Clayton Highlanders 1pt Higham 6pts

CUMBERWORTH v
OLD ALMONDBURIANS
OLD ALMONDBURIANS
Taylor (JD) lbw b Kilner 0
Bradley b Kilner 0
Taylor (T) st Hirst b Haigh 20
Slack c and b Greaves 4
Childs b Greaves 16
Atkinson b Haigh 0
Tunnacliffe c Senior (Sam) b
    McNaught 54

1997 – The club's 14th Huddersfield Central League championship.

CHAPTER 12
TOWARDS WAKEFIELD: EMLEY AND FLOCKTON

Two South Kirklees clubs, in particular, have strong Wakefield connections: Emley and Flockton. In the early days Emley Cricket Club had links with the village football club. This continued on into the last decade of the twentieth century. Now rugby is played on the pitch adjoining the cricket field. Emley Nonconformists also flew the flag for the village on the cricket field. Flockton, like Emley, is an old mining community and the story is told that the village cricket club, building a ground in the 1920s, was helped by the fact that in 1926 most local people were not working because of the General Strike, and so work on the ground progressed quite rapidly.

This unknown Emley cricketer is wearing fascinating attire: cap, tie and black pads! Moreover, his bat looks like it has seen plenty of wear and tear.

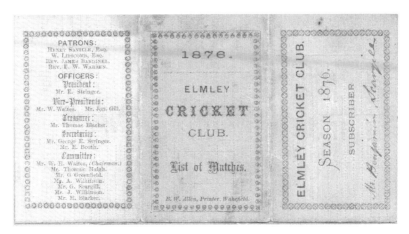

This is the oldest surviving membership card – 1876. Note the presence of three clergymen among the club patrons and the generally hierarchical nature of the club as an organisation. In 1876 Emley was actually spelt Elmley!

This team photograph is revealing. It highlights the kaleidoscopic nature of cricketing attire in the late nineteenth century and the role of the local vicar, Rev. Edward Sutton – seated in the middle at the front.

An Emley cricketer sat in the Coronation float that toured the village in 1953.

When club secretary Mrs Moxon retired after 40 years of service, she was presented with a special gift.

FLOCKTON V. MIRFIELD.

A match was played on Saturday, the 20th of June, at Flockton, when the home club won by nine runs. Decided by first innings. The following is the score:—

FLOCKTON.

First Innings.   Second Innings.
George Hewitt, c and b Smith   5
Alfred Radford, b Broadbent ...   3   not out............   4
George Vokes, c and b Smithson   12   not out............   27
C. Armitage, c Schofield b Broad-
  bent......................   3   b Smithson   13
H. W. Stansfield, b Smithson   6   b Broadbent ...   12
Richard Walker, b Smithson   0   b Broadbent ...   5
Henry Pickard, b Broadbent   2
Joseph Armitage, b Smithson   0
Thomas Leather, c Pickering b
  Smithson   8
Arthur Bedford, not out   4   b Broadbent ...   10
James Bradley, c Smithson b
  Broadbent   5
  Extras.................   7   Extras.....   17
                                  ---   ---
        Total.............   55   Total....   88

MIRFIELD.

P. Smithson, c C. Armitage b Hewitt   6
H. Broadbent, b Hewitt   4
J. Horner, b Armitage   1
R. T. Horner, b Armitage   1
J. R. Moffatt, c Leather b Hewitt   3
J. Pickering, b Hewitt   8
J. Ledgard, b Armitage   1
A. Schofield, b Armitage   8
J. Hodge, b Armitage   5
J. Barker, b Hewitt   5
J. Ledgard, not out   1
        Extras   4

        Total   4

FLOCKTON V. THORNHILL.

On Saturday last, the return match was played between these clubs, at Flockton, when the home club won the game by six runs. At Thornhill, Flockton obtained 105 runs against Thornhill's 20 for four wickets down, thus making one win, and one draw greatly in favour. The fielding and stumping (especially T. Leather) were very good. Pickard, at point, made a splendid catch a good height above him, contorting his body so much by a backward move that, for a time, it was thought he had seriously hurt himself. Score:—

FLOCKTON.

Alfred Bedford, b Crosland   0
George Hewitt, run out   0
George Vokes, l b w, b Crosland...........   6
Richard Walker, b Crosland   0
H. W. Stansfield, b Crosland   16
Arthur Bedford, run out   0
Joseph Armitage, b Crosland   12
Henry Pickard, run out   12
Thomas Leather, not out   1
James Bradley, b Crosland   5
Henry Bloom, st Oates   12
        Extras............................   15

        Total.............................   81

THORNHILL.

C. Firth, c Hewitt b Walker   12
E. Oates, run out   7
R. Ramsden, b Walker   12
H. W. Pace, b Walker......................   9
Thomas Watson, not out   16
W. Crosland, c Pickard b Vokes   5
W. Ellis, run out   0
J. H. Charlesworth, b Vokes   0
W. M. Brown, c Hewitt b Vokes   0
W. Pace, c Arthur Bedford b Vokes   4
W. Butterworth, b Vokes   15
        Extras............................   15

        Total.............................   75

These are two of Flockton's earliest recorded fixtures – in 1868.

118

A pre-1914 Flockton side.

Denby Grange Shield winners in 1935.

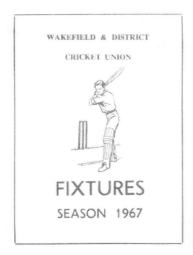

Left: Flockton played in the Wakefield Union before they joined the Huddersfield Central League. Right: 1974 witnessed one of Flockton's great knockout successes.

Yorkshire Cricket Club's first team coach Wayne Clark was the chief guest when the Arrow Huddersfield Central League held their annual dinner and prize presentation evening at Painthorpe Country Club. 325 guests attended the evening, with entertainment provided by Malcolm Lord, who was MC, and comedian Austin Knight. The main presentation of the night, the Fred Stallard Trophy, for services to a club and the league, went to Flockton's Harry Marsden, who has been secretary and treasurer for 30 years, groundsman for the past 25, and a member of the League's Management Board for 12 years, as well as a player. Wayne Clark is pictured with the County Championship Trophy (third left) with (from left): Chris Taylor and Robert Hills, from League sponsors Arrow, president Adrian Whittaker, Harry Marsden and secretary Jack Carson

Harry Marsden is 'Mr Flockton CC' – the epitome of a local cricket club stalwart. Here he is being presented with the Fred Stallard Trophy by officials of the Huddersfield Central Cricket League – due recognition of his services to the game.

INDEX

Acre Mills CC 23
Allsop, Friend 92, 97
Allsop Cup 97, 98, 99, 106
Almondbury 35
Almondbury CC 35-38
Almondbury Casuals CC 35
Almondbury Wesleyan Athletic Club 39
Almondbury Wesleyans CC 35, 38-41
Almondbury Zion CC 38
Ambepitia, Gunasiri 28
Arkenley Lane 41, 42
Armitage Bridge 67
Armitage Bridge CC 67, 70-71, 72
Armitage Fold 70
Association Challenge Cup 77
Augustinians CC 31-32

Balderstone, Chris 17
Ball, Polly 47
Bamforth, H 81
Bankfield 8
Barbados 20
Barker, J. 82
Bates, Billy 50
BBC Radio 4 75
Beaumont, Ralph 71
Beaumont, W. 65
Berry, George 1
Berry, John 1
Berry, Joseph 1
Birchencliffe 23
Birchencliffe CC 33
Birchencliffe Church CC 33
Birkby 23
Birkby CYC CC 23
Birkby FMA CC 25, 26-27
Birkby St. John's CC 23
Birkby United CC 23
Bolt, Billy 6
Booth, Andy 45
Booth, Joyce 76

Bradbury, Johnny 30
Bradley & Colnebridge CC 1, 11-12
Bradley Mills CC 1, 6-7, 8
Bradley Mills Working Men's Club 1
Bramall Lane 49
Brennan, Colin 26
Britannia Works CC 25
Britannia Works Cricket Ground 25
Britannia Works Sports Club 25
Broad Oak CC 56, 64-66
Byrom Shield 19, 84

Cartworth Moor 79
Cartworth Moor CC 87-88
Castle, J. 35
Castle Hill 35, 43
Challenge Shield 25
Chaterton, Leslie 25
Clayton West 100
Clayton West CC 113-114
Close, Brian 40
Colne & Holme Valley League 62
Colne Valley League 21, 56
Colne Valley Male Voice Choir 56
Colne Valley Museum 56
Constantine, Learie 59
Coronation float 117
Cowrakes Road 23
Crossland, Andrew 1, 3
Crossland, Joseph 1
Crossland Trophy 25
Crum, Jack 70
Cumberworth 92
Cumberworth Lane 98
Cumberworth Steppes 99
Cumberworth United CC 97-99, 107

D'Oliveira, Basil 57
Dalton CC 1-2
Dalton Wesleyans CC 1
Dawson, George 61, 82
Dawson, Jim 78

Dearne Valley League 105, 113
Defreitas, Phil 104
Deighton 1, 12
Denby 92
Denby CC 95-97
Denby Dale 87, 92
Denby Dale CC 92-94
Denby Dale Pie Hall 92
Denby Grange Shield 119
Denby United CC 95
Derbyshire 85
Digley Mills CC 79
Dolley, Alan 27
Dolley, Brian 27
Dolley, Julie 27
Doshi, Dilip 83
Dowling, R. 42
Dunford Bridge 90

Edgerton CC 2, 23, 25, 29-30
Elland CC 17
Elmley 116
Emley 115
Emley CC 111, 115-117
Emley FC 115
Emley Nonconformists CC 115
Eyre, Peter 19

Fartown, 1, 4, 5, 6, 8, 53, 54, 63,
Fernside Avenue 36, 38
First World War 38, 68
Firth, David 97
Flockton 115
Flockton CC 118-120
Foster, John 15

Gavaskar, Sunil 110
General Strike 115
Gentlemen of Golcar CC 15
Gill Lane 87
Golcar Band 22
Golcar Church Institute CC 15
Golcar CC 15, 18-20,
Golcar Liberal CC 15
Golcar Sing 18

Golcar Treasurer's XI CC 15
Grasscroft, Honley 67

Haigh, Bob 106, 111
Halifax 23
Halifax League 24
Halifax Road, Birchencliffe 23
Hall Bower CC 43-45
Harry Lime CC 25
Heavy Woollen Cup 37, 51
Helme CC 84
Hemplow, Marsden 56
Heywood, Geoff 45
Highfields, Edgerton 29, 30
Hill Top, Slaithwaite 60
Hill, Allen 50
'Hillites' 46
Hinchcliffe, Zachariah 92
Hinchliffe, Harry 65
Hinchliffe Cup 46
Hirst, George Herbert 1, 3, 8, 10,
14
Holden Cup 88
Holmbridge 79, 85
Holmbridge CC 85-86
Holmebridge Britannia CC 85
Holmes, Percy 16
Holmfirth 79, 85, 87, 91
Holmfirth CC 79-81
Honley 67
Honley CC 67, 68-69
Honley Congregationals CC 67
Honley Wesleyans CC 67
Huddersfield 49, 67, 97
Huddersfield Alliance League 44,
103
Huddersfield & District Evening
League 24
Huddersfield & Lockwood CC 1
Huddersfield Association 11, 12,
19, 24, 25, 26, 27, 29, 30, 31, 33,
40
Huddersfield Canal 6

Huddersfield Central League 2, 21, 23, 24, 44, 45, 75, 85, 89, 91, 96, 97, 105, 114
Huddersfield Clarence CC 1
Huddersfield C&AC 1, 3-5, 72
Huddersfield Cricket Festival 4
Huddersfield League 19, 43, 45, 46, 53, 55, 63, 65, 72, 76, 78, 81, 83, 97, 105, 120
Huddersfield Police 73
Huddersfield Town FC 45
Huddersfield United CC 1, 14
'Huddersfield Vagabonds' 30
Huddersfield Wanderers CC 1, 14
Huddersfield Youth Association CC 1
Huddersfield Examiner 16, 43, 63
Hutton, Len 71, 86

ICI CC 1
Inniss, Stanley 13
Inter-Caribbean CC 1
International CC 26
Iqbal, Riaz 28

Jakeman, Bruce 69

Kaye Lane 38, 40
King James' School 41
'King Willow's Haunts' 63
Kirkburton 100, 104
Kirkburton CC 55, 102-104
Kirkheaton CC 1, 8-10, 102
Kirklees Race Relations Board 13
Kirklees Way 99

Ladies Committee 48
Lancashire 56
Lascelles Hall CC 1, 37, 49-55, 56
Last of the Summer Wine, 79
Laund Hill 32
Lawrence Batley Sports Centre 32
Leadbeater, Eddie 13, 36
Leeds Road 6
Lepton 100, 102

Lepton Highlanders CC 100-101
Leymoor CC 15
Leymoor United CC 21-22
Lindley 23
Lindley Church CC 23
Lindley CC 23
Lindley Parish Church CC 87
Linthwaite 56
Linthwaite CC 56, 62-64
Linthwaite Hall CC 56
Little Hayfield CC 85
Littlewood, Roger 112
Lockwood 67
Lockwood CC 72
Lockwood, Ephraim 50
Lockwood Viaduct 70
Lodge, Alec 55
Lodge, E.A. 51
Longley Park Golf Club 42
Longroyd Bridge 16
Lord's Cricket Ground 19
Lower Denby 95
Luddism 56
Lumb Cup 12, 13, 19, 25, 26, 28, 40, 46, 77, 84

MacLean, Jock 25
Marsden 56
Marsden CC 56-58
Marsden Mechanics Institute CC 56
Marsden, Harry 120
Marsh 23
Marsh CC 23
Marsh Lane, Shepley 110
Martins CC 23
Mean Lane, Meltham 83
Meltham 79
Meltham CC 53, 82-83
Meltham Mills CC 35, 84
Milnsbridge Baptists CC 15
Milnsbridge CYC CC 15
Milnsbridge Socialist Band 16
Milnsbridge Wesleyans CC 15
Mirfield CC 118

Miry Lane 78
Moldgreen CC 43
'Moonraking' 56
Moorhouse family 71
Moxon, Howard 97
Moxon, Mrs 117

National Lottery 92
New Hey Road 23, 25
North Stars CC (Barbados) 20
Nortonthorpe 100
Nortonthorpe CC 98, 111-112

Oakes 23
Oakes Baptists CC 23
Oakes CYC 23
Oakes Council School 16
Old Almondburians CC 35, 41-42
Old Almondburians Society 41
Old Boys CC 23
Ossett CC 37

Pack Horse Hotel 53
Paddock CC 15-18, 83
Paddock CYC CC 15
Paddock CYC OB CC 15
Paddock Institute CC 15
Paddock Methodist Church 15
Paddock Rangers 15
Paddock Shield 58
Parkin, Harold 45
Penistone & District League 96
Penistone, Parish of 96
'Pip Hillers' 46
'Pips' 46
Pole Moor CC 23
Primrose Hill CC 43, 46-48

Ramadhin, Sonny 15, 19, 20
Rastrick CC 53
Rhodes, Wilfred 1, 8, 10, 14
Rochdale 23
Rose Hill Reporter 29
Rowley Hill CC 100, 102
Royal Hotel 33

St Hill, Edwin 60
St John's Golcar CC 18
Salendine Nook 23
Salendine Nook Baptists CC 23
Salendine Nook Old Boys CC 24-25
Scholes 79
Scholes CC 89-90
Scissett 100
Second World War 6, 21, 33
Senior, Nigel 99
Senior, Phil 99
Sharpe Rose Bowl 25
Sheepridge & Deighton CC 1
Sheepridge & District League 38
Sheffield CC 49
Shelley 100
Shelley CC 98, 104-105
Shepley 100
Shepley CC 109-110
Skelmanthorpe 100
Skelmanthorpe CC 107-108
Skelmanthorpe Feast 107
Slaithwaite 56
Slaithwaite CC 58-61
Smith, Jerry 26
Snowden, Barry 30
Sobers, Gary 15, 17
Somerset CCC 4
South Yorkshire 97
Stallard Trophy, Fred 120
Storthes Hall 104
Storthes Hall CC 100
Sutton, Rev Edward 116
Sykes Cup 9, 16, 19, 37, 45, 53, 55, 58, 63, 65, 69, 83

Taylor, Jack 41, 42
Taylor, Ken 47
Thackray's XI, E. 107
Thewlis, John 50
Thongsbridge 67
Thongsbridge CC 77-78
Thornhill CC 118
Thurstonland 67

Thurstonland CC 74-76, 97
Tinker Cup 112
Tolson Museum, Huddersfield 13
Topp, A. 82
Tottenham Hotspur FC 45
Town End, Golcar 18

United North of England XI 80
Upper Denby 95
Upperthong 79
Upperthong CC 91

Victoria Tower 43

Wakefield 115
Wakefield & District Union 120
Wakefield Road, Denby Dale 94
Walkers Arms 22
Warrenside, Deighton 12
Washington, J., 65
Watson, Willie 16, 17
West Indians CC 1, 13,
West View, Paddock 15, 18
Westwood United CC 62
Women's cricket 5, 86, 92
Woodfield Park Police Sports CC
73
Wool Pack Hotel, Almondbury 35

YMCA CC 27
Yorkshire CCC 1, 4, 16, 19, 40, 49,
54